GPU Mastery

Advanced Architectures, Evolution, and Cutting-Edge Applications in Gaming & Machine Learning.

©

Written By

Maxime Lane

GPU Mastery: Advanced Architectures, Evolution, and Cutting-Edge Applications in Gaming & Machine Learning
Copyright © 2025 by Maxime lane

Published in United States by Maxime Lane

This is a work of nonfiction. The names, characters, businesses, organizations, events, locales, and incidents portrayed in this book are either the products of the author's imagination or used in a fictitious manner. Any resemblance to actual persons, living or dead, or actual events is purely coincidental.

First Edition

Disclaimer:
The information provided in this book is for general informational purposes only. While every effort has been made to ensure the accuracy of the information presented, neither the publisher nor the author assumes any responsibility for errors or omissions, or for the results obtained from the use of this information. All information in this book is provided "as is," with no guarantee of completeness, accuracy, timeliness, or of the results obtained from the use of this information, and without warranty of any kind, express or implied.

Table of Content

Foreword

In the ever-evolving world of technology, GPUs have transitioned from simple graphics accelerators to complex engines powering high-performance computing, advanced gaming, and groundbreaking machine learning applications. I am honored to introduce **"GPU Mastery: Advanced Architectures, Evolution, and Cutting-Edge Applications in Gaming & Machine Learning."**

This book is the culmination of years of research, practical experimentation, and collaboration among experts in the field. It bridges the gap between theoretical frameworks and real-world applications, offering readers an in-depth exploration of GPU architectures, from the fundamentals to the innovations that define today's and tomorrow's computing landscapes.

As you delve into these pages, you will discover clear explanations, hands-on examples, and detailed case studies that make complex topics accessible. Whether you are a seasoned professional or a researcher looking to deepen your understanding, this book will serve as both a reference and a roadmap for harnessing the full potential of modern GPUs.

I commend the author for his dedication and meticulous attention to detail. May this work inspire you to push the boundaries of what is possible in high-performance computing and creative technology.

Preface

Welcome to **"GPU Mastery: Advanced Architectures, Evolution, and Cutting-Edge Applications in Gaming & Machine Learning."** This book was conceived with the goal of creating a definitive resource for advanced users and professionals who wish to master the intricacies of GPU technology.

Goals of This Book

- **Deep Technical Understanding:**
  We aim to unravel the complexities of GPU architectures, covering everything from fundamental principles to the latest advancements. Detailed explanations and clear diagrams are provided to demystify even the most challenging topics.
- **Historical and Evolutionary Insights:**
  Understanding how GPU technology has evolved over time is key to appreciating its current state and future potential. This book includes comprehensive historical context and discusses critical milestones in GPU development.
- **Practical Applications:**
  Through extensive hands-on examples, case studies, and practical code snippets, we demonstrate how advanced GPUs are applied in high-end gaming engines and machine learning frameworks. You will learn not just the theory, but also how to implement and optimize GPU-driven applications.

Scope and Intended Audience

This book is written for:

- **Advanced Users:**
  Professionals who already have a background in computing or hardware design and wish to deepen their technical knowledge of GPU architectures.
- **Industry Professionals and Researchers:**
  Those working in high-performance computing, game development, or artificial intelligence will find real-world examples, case studies, and best practices to apply in their projects.

- **Educators and Students:**
  Academics looking for a comprehensive reference to support advanced coursework or research in GPU technology.

By combining thorough research, clear language, and practical insights, we hope to make this book a cornerstone for anyone serious about mastering GPU technology.

Acknowledgments

Creating a resource of this depth and breadth would not have been possible without the support and contributions of many individuals and institutions. We would like to express our sincere gratitude to:

- **The Peer Reviewers:**
  Our heartfelt thanks to the panel of experts who rigorously reviewed each chapter, ensuring the technical accuracy and clarity of the content. Their insightful comments and constructive feedback have been invaluable.
- **Academic and Research Institutions:**
  We are grateful to the GPU Research Lab and the Department of Computer Engineering at our respective universities for providing access to cutting-edge research, state-of-the-art facilities, and an environment of innovation.
- **Industry Partners:**
  Special thanks to the professionals at NVIDIA, AMD, and Intel who shared their expertise and provided real-world insights that helped shape the practical applications discussed in this book.
- **Colleagues and Friends:**
  To our colleagues and friends in the tech community—your encouragement and willingness to share knowledge have made this journey both rewarding and enriching.
- **Family and Loved Ones:**
  Last but not least, thank you to our families for their unwavering support, understanding, and patience throughout the writing and research process.

Each contribution, large or small, has played a part in making this work as comprehensive and accessible as it is today.

Chapter 1: Introduction to GPUs in Modern Computing

This chapter sets the stage for understanding how Graphics Processing Units (GPUs) have transformed over time—from specialized hardware designed exclusively for rendering images to versatile, powerful compute engines that drive modern computing tasks. In this chapter, we explore the emergence of GPUs and provide a historical timeline of their evolution, outlining key milestones that have shaped their development.

1.1 The Emergence of GPUs

From Graphics Accelerators to Compute Engines

In the early days of personal computing, the main focus was on Central Processing Units (CPUs) that handled general-purpose computations. However, as computer graphics became increasingly important—especially with the rise of video games and multimedia applications—there was a clear need for dedicated hardware that could handle complex graphical operations quickly and efficiently. This need led to the development of the first generation of graphics accelerators.

Early Graphics Accelerators

Early graphics accelerators were specialized circuits designed to offload image rendering tasks from the CPU. Their primary purpose was to manage operations such as drawing lines, filling polygons, and applying textures. These devices worked in tandem with the CPU, handling specific tasks that required rapid computation and high-speed memory access. Although their functionality was limited compared to modern GPUs, they were critical in improving the visual experience in computer games and graphical user interfaces.

The Transition to GPUs

Over time, the evolution of computer graphics and the increasing complexity of visual effects pushed the capabilities of these accelerators further. Developers began to integrate programmable elements into the hardware, enabling a shift from fixed-function pipelines to more flexible, programmable architectures. This transition allowed for greater customization and the development of techniques such as shader programming, which enabled dynamic lighting, realistic shadows, and other advanced graphical effects.

As these programmable units became more sophisticated, GPUs evolved into devices capable not only of rendering complex graphics but also of performing massive parallel computations. Researchers and engineers soon discovered that the highly parallel structure of GPUs made them ideal for tasks beyond graphics processing. They could handle matrix operations, data parallel algorithms, and other compute-intensive tasks more efficiently than traditional CPUs. This realization paved the way for GPUs to become essential compute engines in fields such as scientific computing, machine learning, and data analytics.

Key Characteristics of Modern GPUs

Modern GPUs are defined by several key features:

- **Massive Parallelism:** With thousands of cores designed for parallel processing, GPUs excel at handling large volumes of simultaneous computations.
- **High Throughput:** Designed for fast, efficient data processing, GPUs manage high-speed data transfer between memory and compute units.
- **Programmability:** The shift from fixed-function to programmable pipelines allows developers to create custom algorithms and applications tailored to specific computational needs.
- **Versatility:** Today's GPUs are used not only in rendering graphics but also in accelerating complex computations across various scientific and industrial applications.

These characteristics have transformed GPUs from simple graphics accelerators into indispensable components of modern computing systems.

1.2 Historical Overview: From Graphics to General-Purpose Computing

Understanding the evolution of GPUs requires looking back at the key developments and milestones that have defined their journey. The following timeline highlights some of the most significant events in the history of GPU technology.

Timeline of Critical Milestones in GPU Development

Year	Milestone	Description
1980s	**Early Graphics Accelerators**	Dedicated hardware began to emerge to handle 2D graphics rendering tasks, significantly offloading the CPU.
1990	**Introduction of 3D Graphics**	The shift to 3D graphics necessitated more complex hardware, leading to the development of early 3D accelerators. Companies like ATI and NVIDIA started experimenting with more advanced architectures.
1999	**NVIDIA GeForce 256**	Often regarded as the first true GPU, the GeForce 256 introduced hardware transformation and lighting (T&L), marking a major leap in graphics processing capabilities.
2000s	**Programmable Shaders**	The introduction of programmable shader units allowed developers to write custom code for pixel and vertex processing, greatly enhancing graphical realism and opening the door to more versatile applications.
2006	**CUDA and General-Purpose GPU Computing**	NVIDIA's CUDA platform was launched, enabling developers to harness the GPU for tasks beyond graphics rendering. This was a turning point that expanded the role of GPUs to include scientific computing and data processing.
2010s	**Rise of Deep Learning and AI**	With the advent of deep learning, GPUs became essential for training complex neural networks. Their ability to perform parallel

Year	Milestone	Description
		computations efficiently made them the hardware of choice for machine learning research and applications.
Late 2010s to 2020s	Advanced Architectures and Heterogeneous Computing	Modern GPUs now feature multiple cores, advanced memory hierarchies, and integration with CPU systems. Technologies such as ray tracing and tensor cores have further cemented the GPU's role in both graphics and compute-heavy applications.

Explaining the Milestones

- **Early Graphics Accelerators (1980s):**
  During the 1980s, computer systems relied heavily on CPUs, which struggled to handle the increasingly complex graphical demands of emerging applications. Graphics accelerators were introduced to manage tasks such as drawing and rendering, laying the groundwork for future advancements.
- **Introduction of 3D Graphics (1990):**
  The transition from 2D to 3D graphics required more sophisticated hardware. This era saw the emergence of dedicated 3D accelerators capable of rendering three-dimensional scenes, which were critical for the development of immersive video games and simulations.
- **NVIDIA GeForce 256 (1999):**
  Often celebrated as the first GPU, the GeForce 256 brought hardware transformation and lighting to mainstream computing. This innovation marked the beginning of a new era where GPUs started handling tasks that were once the exclusive domain of CPUs.
- **Programmable Shaders (2000s):**
  The introduction of programmable shaders revolutionized the field of computer graphics. Developers could now write custom programs to control the way pixels and vertices were processed, leading to more dynamic and realistic visual effects.
- **CUDA and General-Purpose GPU Computing (2006):**
  With the launch of CUDA, NVIDIA unlocked the potential of GPUs for general-purpose computing. This platform allowed developers to leverage the parallel processing power of GPUs for a wide range of applications, from scientific simulations to complex data analyses.
- **Rise of Deep Learning and AI (2010s):**
  The explosion of deep learning research and applications coincided

with advances in GPU technology. GPUs' ability to perform large-scale parallel computations made them indispensable for training deep neural networks, fundamentally changing the landscape of artificial intelligence.

- **Advanced Architectures and Heterogeneous Computing (Late 2010s to 2020s):**
  Modern GPUs are now at the heart of heterogeneous computing systems, where they work alongside CPUs to provide optimal performance for a variety of tasks. Innovations like ray tracing for photorealistic graphics and tensor cores for deep learning have expanded the role of GPUs far beyond their original purpose.

1.3 The Role of GPUs in Today's Technology Landscape

In today's fast-paced technological environment, GPUs play a crucial role across several high-impact domains. Their design, originally optimized for rendering graphics, now serves as the backbone for many of the most demanding computational tasks. Below, we explore their impact on high-performance computing, gaming, and machine learning.

High-Performance Computing (HPC)

GPUs are increasingly integral to high-performance computing environments. Their inherent ability to perform thousands of calculations in parallel makes them ideal for solving complex scientific and engineering problems. Key applications include:

- **Scientific Simulations:**
  Tasks such as climate modeling, fluid dynamics, and molecular simulations require vast amounts of data to be processed concurrently. GPUs accelerate these simulations by handling multiple data streams simultaneously.
- **Data Analytics:**
  In the era of big data, GPUs help process and analyze enormous datasets quickly. Their parallel architecture significantly reduces the time required for data mining, pattern recognition, and real-time analytics.
- **Financial Modeling:**
  Quantitative finance relies on the rapid computation of risk assessments, option pricing, and market simulations. GPUs provide

the computational muscle needed to run these complex models efficiently.

Example Code Snippet: Parallel Computation with CUDA
Below is a simplified example of how a GPU can be used for parallel computation using NVIDIA's CUDA framework:

cpp

```cpp
// CUDA Kernel to add two arrays
__global__ void addArrays(const float *A, const float *B, float *C, int N) {
    int idx = threadIdx.x + blockIdx.x * blockDim.x;
    if (idx < N) {
        C[idx] = A[idx] + B[idx];
    }
}

// Host code to invoke the kernel
int main() {
    int N = 1024;
    size_t size = N * sizeof(float);

    // Allocate memory on host
    float *h_A = (float *)malloc(size);
    float *h_B = (float *)malloc(size);
    float *h_C = (float *)malloc(size);

    // Initialize host arrays (example initialization)
    for (int i = 0; i < N; i++) {
        h_A[i] = i * 1.0f;
        h_B[i] = (N - i) * 1.0f;
    }

    // Allocate memory on device
    float *d_A, *d_B, *d_C;
    cudaMalloc(&d_A, size);
    cudaMalloc(&d_B, size);
    cudaMalloc(&d_C, size);

    // Copy data from host to device
    cudaMemcpy(d_A, h_A, size, cudaMemcpyHostToDevice);
    cudaMemcpy(d_B, h_B, size, cudaMemcpyHostToDevice);
```

```
// Launch kernel with 256 threads per block
int threadsPerBlock = 256;
int blocksPerGrid = (N + threadsPerBlock - 1) / threadsPerBlock;
addArrays<<<blocksPerGrid, threadsPerBlock>>>(d_A, d_B, d_C, N);

// Copy result from device back to host
cudaMemcpy(h_C, d_C, size, cudaMemcpyDeviceToHost);

// Free device and host memory
cudaFree(d_A);
cudaFree(d_B);
cudaFree(d_C);
free(h_A);
free(h_B);
free(h_C);

    return 0;
}
```

This example demonstrates how a simple addition operation across an array of numbers can be accelerated using parallel processing on a GPU. Although basic, such examples form the building blocks of more sophisticated high-performance applications.

Gaming

The gaming industry has been one of the primary drivers of GPU innovation for decades. Modern games require the rendering of highly detailed, dynamic scenes in real time, and GPUs are engineered to meet these challenges. Their contributions include:

- **Real-Time Rendering:**
  GPUs enable the creation of immersive virtual worlds by rapidly rendering complex graphics, textures, and visual effects. Techniques like shading, lighting, and shadow mapping are handled efficiently by modern GPU architectures.
- **Advanced Visual Effects:**
  With the advent of programmable shaders and real-time ray tracing, GPUs can simulate realistic lighting, reflections, and particle effects that significantly enhance the gaming experience.

- **Virtual Reality (VR) and Augmented Reality (AR):**
  VR and AR applications demand high frame rates and low latency to deliver smooth, interactive experiences. GPUs are essential in processing the high volume of graphical data required for these technologies.

Machine Learning

Machine learning, particularly deep learning, has witnessed a transformative impact due to GPUs. Their parallel processing capabilities allow for the efficient training and inference of neural networks, which are computationally intensive tasks. Key aspects include:

- **Training Neural Networks:**
  Training deep neural networks involves matrix operations and large-scale data processing. GPUs accelerate these computations, reducing training times from weeks to days or even hours.
- **Inference Acceleration:**
  Once a model is trained, GPUs help in deploying it for real-time inference, making applications like image recognition, natural language processing, and autonomous driving feasible in real-world scenarios.
- **Framework Support:**
  Popular machine learning frameworks such as TensorFlow, PyTorch, and MXNet are optimized to take advantage of GPU acceleration. This integration has lowered the barrier to entry for researchers and developers working on complex models.

1.4 Book Structure and How to Use This Guide

This book is designed to be both a comprehensive reference and a practical guide for mastering GPU technology. Here's how the content is organized and how you can best leverage this resource.

Overview of the Book Structure

The book is divided into several major parts, each focusing on different aspects of GPU technology:

1. **Foundations and History:**
   The initial chapters provide a thorough grounding in GPU fundamentals, including their evolution from simple graphics accelerators to modern compute engines. This section sets the stage by covering basic concepts, historical milestones, and the evolution of GPU architecture.
2. **Advanced Architectures and Techniques:**
   Midway through the book, you will find in-depth discussions on the inner workings of modern GPUs. Topics such as parallelism, memory hierarchies, and performance optimizations are explored in detail. These chapters are designed to build on the foundational knowledge and take you into the technical specifics required for advanced applications.
3. **Practical Applications:**
   Subsequent sections focus on real-world applications, particularly in gaming and machine learning. These chapters include practical examples, case studies, and hands-on code samples that demonstrate how GPU technology is applied in various domains.
4. **Future Trends and Emerging Technologies:**
   The final chapters look ahead to the future, discussing emerging trends, next-generation architectures, and the evolving role of GPUs in areas such as artificial intelligence, edge computing, and beyond.
5. **Supplementary Materials:**
   The book also contains appendices and supplementary sections, including a glossary of technical terms, further reading suggestions, and links to interactive online resources. These materials are intended to serve as a quick reference and to provide additional context for deeper exploration.

How to Use This Guide

To get the most out of this book, we recommend the following approach:

- **Sequential Reading for New Concepts:**
  If you are new to some of the advanced topics covered in the book, it is best to read the chapters in sequence. The earlier chapters build a strong foundation, making it easier to understand the more complex subjects discussed later.
- **Hands-On Practice:**
  Throughout the book, you will find code examples, diagrams, and case studies. We encourage you to work through these practical elements actively. Experiment with the provided code, replicate the

experiments, and try modifying them to see how changes affect the results.

- **Use of Supplemental Materials:**
  The appendices and supplementary sections are valuable resources. For instance, the glossary helps clarify technical terms, while the recommended reading list offers avenues for further research. Additionally, online resources linked in the text may include interactive demos and video lectures.
- **Reference for Projects:**
  For professionals and researchers, this book is designed to serve as a detailed reference guide. Whether you're developing a new GPU-accelerated application or optimizing an existing one, the in-depth technical discussions and case studies can be revisited as needed.
- **Interactive Engagement:**
  Where applicable, we have included tables, code examples, and diagrams to clarify complex concepts. Make sure to review these visual aids closely, as they often encapsulate key points in an accessible format.

Example of a Table in the Book:
Below is an example table summarizing the core features of modern GPUs, which you may encounter as a quick reference in your studies:

Feature	Description
Massive Parallelism	Ability to process thousands of tasks concurrently.
High Throughput	Efficient data transfer between memory and processing units.
Programmability	Support for custom algorithms via shader programming.
Versatility	Applicability across graphics, HPC, and machine learning tasks.

By following this guide and actively engaging with the material, you will develop a robust understanding of GPU technology and its applications. Whether you are using this book for self-study, academic research, or professional development, the structured approach and practical examples are designed to help you master both the theory and practice of modern GPUs.

Chapter 2: Fundamentals of GPU Architecture

In this chapter, we delve into the essential principles underlying GPU architecture and contrast them with traditional CPU designs. Understanding these fundamentals will provide you with the necessary background to appreciate the strengths and limitations of GPUs, as well as their role in modern computing systems.

2.1 Core Design Principles of GPUs

Modern GPUs are engineered to handle a vast number of simultaneous operations, making them well-suited for tasks that benefit from parallel processing. Let's break down the key building blocks of GPU architecture.

2.1.1 Streaming Multiprocessors (SMs) and Compute Cores

At the heart of a GPU are Streaming Multiprocessors (SMs) (or Compute Units in some architectures). Each SM consists of multiple smaller processing cores that work in parallel to execute thousands of threads concurrently.

- **Parallelism:**
  GPUs are designed to execute many threads simultaneously. Each SM can handle hundreds of threads, which is crucial for workloads like graphics rendering and neural network computations.
- **SIMT Architecture:**
  GPUs typically employ a Single Instruction, Multiple Threads (SIMT) architecture. This means that one instruction is broadcast to many cores, which execute that instruction on different data elements simultaneously.

2.1.2 Memory Hierarchy

The efficiency of a GPU is not solely dependent on its compute cores but also on its sophisticated memory hierarchy:

- **Global Memory:**
  This is the main memory available on the GPU. It is large in capacity but has higher latency compared to on-chip memory. Data required for computations is typically loaded from global memory.
- **Shared Memory / L1 Cache:**
  Each SM has a small, fast shared memory that all cores within the SM can access quickly. This memory is used to store data that needs to be shared among threads, significantly reducing the latency involved in accessing global memory.
- **Registers:**
  Registers are the fastest memory available and are used to store data that is immediately required for computation. Each core has its own set of registers, ensuring rapid access and low latency.
- **Constant and Texture Memory:**
  Specialized memory types optimized for specific types of access patterns (e.g., constant values or textures in graphics applications) further enhance performance in certain scenarios.

2.1.3 Threading and Concurrency

GPUs are optimized for massive concurrency:

- **Thread Blocks and Grids:**
  In programming models like CUDA, threads are organized into blocks, and blocks are organized into a grid. This structure allows for scalable parallelism across thousands of threads.
- **Latency Hiding:**
  Due to the high latency of global memory access, GPUs use thread scheduling to switch between threads. While some threads wait for data from memory, others are scheduled to execute, ensuring the compute units are always busy.

2.1.4 Specialized Hardware Units

Modern GPUs include specialized hardware that caters to particular tasks:

- **Texture Units:**
  These are designed to efficiently handle texture mapping, filtering, and other operations critical to image processing.
- **Tensor Cores:**
  Found in recent GPU architectures, tensor cores are optimized for matrix operations, which are central to deep learning algorithms.

They provide significant acceleration for operations like convolution and matrix multiplication.
- **Ray Tracing Cores:**
  Some modern GPUs include dedicated hardware for ray tracing, allowing for more realistic lighting and shadows in real-time graphics.

Example: Visualizing a GPU's Basic Architecture

Below is a simplified diagram illustrating the core components of a typical GPU:

sql

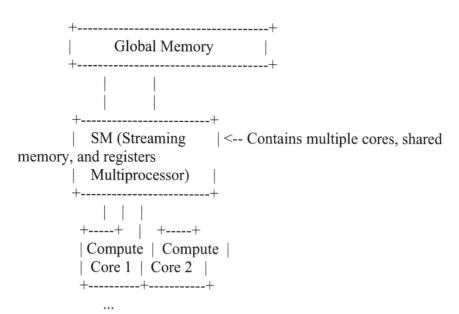

```
        +-----------------------------------+
        |          Global Memory            |
        +-----------------------------------+
            |       |
            |       |
        +------------------------+
        |   SM (Streaming        | <-- Contains multiple cores, shared
memory, and registers
        |   Multiprocessor)      |
        +------------------------+
            |  |  |
        +-----+  |  +-----+
        | Compute  | Compute |
        | Core 1  | Core 2  |
        +----------+----------+
            ...
```

This diagram highlights how compute cores within an SM access shared memory and registers, with the entire GPU accessing the larger, slower global memory.

2.2 Comparing GPUs and CPUs

While both GPUs and CPUs are critical to computing systems, they have distinct architectures optimized for different types of tasks. Understanding these differences is crucial for leveraging each processor's strengths.

2.2.1 Architectural Differences

Feature	CPU	GPU
Core Count	Few cores (typically 4–16) optimized for sequential processing	Hundreds to thousands of simpler cores optimized for parallel tasks
Instruction Handling	Complex control logic, supports a wide range of instructions	Simplified control logic with a focus on executing the same instruction across many cores (SIMT)
Memory Hierarchy	Deep cache hierarchies (L1, L2, L3) designed for latency reduction	High-bandwidth memory interfaces with smaller caches and fast shared memory within SMs
Execution Model	Designed for low-latency, single-threaded performance	Designed for high throughput with simultaneous multi-threading
Task Suitability	General-purpose tasks, sequential operations, complex decision trees	Data-parallel tasks, vectorized operations, compute-intensive workloads

2.2.2 Complementary Roles in Modern Systems

- **CPUs:**
  CPUs excel in handling a broad range of tasks that require sequential processing, complex control flows, and quick responses to changing program conditions. They are ideal for running operating systems, managing system resources, and executing tasks that cannot be easily parallelized.
- **GPUs:**
  GPUs shine in scenarios where large amounts of data can be processed in parallel. They are essential for:
    - **Graphics Rendering:** Rapidly processing millions of pixels and vertices to create smooth, high-quality images.
    - **Scientific Computation:** Handling large-scale simulations and data analysis that benefit from parallel execution.
    - **Machine Learning:** Accelerating the training and inference of deep neural networks by performing numerous mathematical operations concurrently.

2.2.3 A Practical Example: Image Processing

Consider a simple image processing task, such as applying a filter to an image. This task can be efficiently parallelized, making it a good candidate for GPU acceleration.

CPU Implementation (Simplified Pseudocode):

python

```python
# Pseudocode for applying a filter to an image using CPU
def apply_filter_cpu(image, filter_kernel):
    height, width = image.shape
    output = create_empty_image(height, width)
    for i in range(height):
        for j in range(width):
            # Apply filter to each pixel
            output[i][j] = compute_filtered_value(image, filter_kernel, i, j)
    return output
```

GPU Implementation (Simplified CUDA-like Pseudocode):

cpp

```cpp
// CUDA kernel for applying a filter to an image
__global__ void applyFilterGPU(const unsigned char *image, unsigned char *output, const float *filter, int width, int height) {
    int x = blockIdx.x * blockDim.x + threadIdx.x;
    int y = blockIdx.y * blockDim.y + threadIdx.y;
    if (x < width && y < height) {
        float pixelValue = 0.0f;
        // Loop over the filter kernel (assuming a 3x3 filter for simplicity)
        for (int fx = -1; fx <= 1; fx++) {
            for (int fy = -1; fy <= 1; fy++) {
                int imageX = min(max(x + fx, 0), width - 1);
                int imageY = min(max(y + fy, 0), height - 1);
                pixelValue += image[imageY * width + imageX] * filter[(fy + 1) * 3 + (fx + 1)];
            }
        }
        output[y * width + x] = (unsigned char) pixelValue;
    }
```

}

// Host code to launch the GPU kernel would handle memory allocation, copying data, and invoking the kernel.

Explanation:

- In the **CPU implementation**, the image is processed pixel by pixel in a nested loop. Each pixel's new value is computed sequentially.
- In the **GPU implementation**, each thread is responsible for processing one pixel. Threads are organized into a two-dimensional grid corresponding to the image dimensions. This approach allows thousands of pixels to be processed concurrently, dramatically speeding up the computation.

2.2.4 Summary of Differences

- **Performance:**
  For tasks that can be broken down into many small, independent operations, GPUs offer superior performance due to their parallel processing capabilities. In contrast, CPUs excel at handling complex, sequential tasks.
- **Flexibility:**
  CPUs provide greater flexibility and are capable of handling a wider range of operations, while GPUs are specialized for high-throughput, data-parallel computations.

2.3 Key Components: Compute Units, Memory Hierarchy, and Interconnects

In this section, we take a deep dive into the critical components that define modern GPU performance. We will explore compute units—including shader cores, the intricate memory hierarchy (caches, shared memory, and registers), and the interconnects that link these elements.

Compute Units and Shader Cores

Compute Units (CUs), sometimes referred to as **Streaming Multiprocessors (SMs)** in NVIDIA terminology, are the workhorses of a

GPU. Each compute unit contains multiple smaller cores (often called **shader cores** or **CUDA cores**) that execute instructions in parallel.

- **Shader Cores:**
  These are specialized processing units designed for handling graphics computations such as shading, lighting, and texture mapping. In modern GPUs, shader cores have evolved to support general-purpose computing tasks. Their architecture is optimized for executing the same instruction across many data elements simultaneously—a model known as **Single Instruction, Multiple Threads (SIMT)**.
- **Parallel Execution:**
  The large number of shader cores allows GPUs to process thousands of threads concurrently. This design is ideal for tasks like rendering complex scenes in real time or performing large-scale matrix operations in machine learning.

Memory Hierarchy

The memory architecture of a GPU is carefully designed to balance speed, size, and cost. Understanding this hierarchy is essential for optimizing performance.

Levels of GPU Memory

1. **Global Memory:**
   - **Description:**
     This is the largest memory pool available on the GPU and is accessible by all compute units.
   - **Characteristics:**
     High capacity but relatively high latency.
   - **Usage:**
     Stores data that is shared across many threads and is often the source of input data for computations.
2. **Shared Memory / L1 Cache:**
   - **Description:**
     Each compute unit features a small, fast memory region shared among all its cores.
   - **Characteristics:**
     Low latency and high bandwidth.

- o **Usage:**
  Ideal for data that is repeatedly accessed by threads within the same block. This memory is critical for reducing the frequency of global memory accesses.
3. **Registers:**
   - o **Description:**
     Registers are the fastest form of memory and are local to each core.
   - o **Characteristics:**
     Extremely low latency.
   - o **Usage:**
     Used to store immediate variables and intermediate computation results.
4. **Constant and Texture Memory:**
   - o **Description:**
     Specialized memory areas optimized for certain access patterns.
   - o **Characteristics:**
     Lower latency when accessed correctly, often with caching strategies optimized for specific workloads.
   - o **Usage:**
     Constant memory is ideal for read-only data that does not change over the course of kernel execution, while texture memory is optimized for spatial locality in image processing tasks.

Memory Hierarchy Summary Table

Memory Type	Capacity	Latency	Bandwidth	Typical Usage
Global Memory	High (GBs)	High	Moderate	Bulk data storage, input/output for kernels
Shared Memory / L1 Cache	Moderate (tens of KB per SM)	Low	High	Inter-thread communication, frequently accessed data
Registers	Low (KB per core)	Very Low	Very High	Immediate variables, temporary computation results

Memory Type	Capacity	Latency	Bandwidth	Typical Usage
Constant Memory	Low to Moderate	Low (with caching)	High (when cached)	Read-only parameters, constants
Texture Memory	Variable	Low (with caching)	Optimized for spatial data	Image data, texture mapping in graphics applications

Interconnects and Bus Architectures

Interconnects are the communication pathways that link different components of the GPU as well as connect the GPU to the CPU and other system resources.

- **Internal Interconnects:**
  Within the GPU, high-speed buses and crossbar switches are used to connect compute units with memory controllers, ensuring data moves rapidly between cores and various memory hierarchies.
- **External Interconnects:**
  - **PCI Express (PCIe):**
    The most common interface for connecting GPUs to the host system. It provides a high-speed data channel between the GPU and CPU.
  - **NVLink:**
    Developed by NVIDIA, NVLink offers significantly higher bandwidth compared to PCIe. It is used for GPU-to-GPU communication and for linking GPUs with CPUs in specialized high-performance systems.
- **Importance of Interconnects:**
  The speed and efficiency of these interconnects are crucial for overall system performance. Bottlenecks in data transfer can negate the advantages of high computational throughput.

2.4 Introduction to GPU Programming Models

To harness the power of GPU architectures, developers rely on specialized programming models that abstract the hardware complexities and allow efficient parallel computation. In this section, we introduce the most widely used GPU programming models: CUDA, OpenCL, and emerging paradigms.

CUDA (Compute Unified Device Architecture)

Developed by NVIDIA, **CUDA** is a parallel computing platform and programming model that provides a C/C++ based language for writing programs that execute on NVIDIA GPUs.

- **Key Features:**
  - Direct access to GPU's virtual instruction set.
  - Extensive libraries and tools for debugging and performance profiling.
  - Strong community and rich documentation.
- **Basic Structure of a CUDA Program:**

cpp

```cpp
// Example: Vector addition using CUDA

// CUDA kernel definition
__global__ void vectorAdd(const float *A, const float *B, float *C, int N) {
    int idx = threadIdx.x + blockDim.x * blockIdx.x;
    if (idx < N) {
        C[idx] = A[idx] + B[idx];
    }
}

int main() {
    int N = 1024;
    size_t size = N * sizeof(float);

    // Allocate host memory
    float *h_A = (float *)malloc(size);
    float *h_B = (float *)malloc(size);
    float *h_C = (float *)malloc(size);

    // Initialize host arrays
    for (int i = 0; i < N; i++) {
```

```
        h_A[i] = i * 1.0f;
        h_B[i] = (N - i) * 1.0f;
    }

    // Allocate device memory
    float *d_A, *d_B, *d_C;
    cudaMalloc(&d_A, size);
    cudaMalloc(&d_B, size);
    cudaMalloc(&d_C, size);

    // Copy data to device
    cudaMemcpy(d_A, h_A, size, cudaMemcpyHostToDevice);
    cudaMemcpy(d_B, h_B, size, cudaMemcpyHostToDevice);

    // Launch kernel: each block contains 256 threads
    int threadsPerBlock = 256;
    int blocksPerGrid = (N + threadsPerBlock - 1) / threadsPerBlock;
    vectorAdd<<<blocksPerGrid, threadsPerBlock>>>(d_A, d_B,
d_C, N);

    // Copy result back to host
    cudaMemcpy(h_C, d_C, size, cudaMemcpyDeviceToHost);

    // Free memory
    cudaFree(d_A);
    cudaFree(d_B);
    cudaFree(d_C);
    free(h_A);
    free(h_B);
    free(h_C);

    return 0;
}
```

Explanation:
In this example, a simple vector addition is performed. The kernel
vectorAdd runs on the GPU, where each thread computes the sum of
corresponding elements in arrays A and B. This code demonstrates
the basic structure of a CUDA program, including memory
allocation, data transfer, kernel execution, and cleanup.

OpenCL (Open Computing Language)

OpenCL is an open standard for parallel programming across diverse hardware platforms, including GPUs from different vendors, CPUs, and other processors.

- **Key Features:**
    - Platform-agnostic: Supports multiple hardware architectures.
    - C-based programming language with extensions for parallel computing.
    - Enables heterogeneous computing by allowing the same code to run on various devices.
- **Basic Structure of an OpenCL Program:**

Although similar in concept to CUDA, OpenCL requires setting up a context, compiling kernels at runtime, and managing command queues. Here's a very high-level pseudocode outline:

c

```c
// Pseudocode for an OpenCL kernel
__kernel void vectorAdd(__global const float *A,
                __global const float *B,
                __global float *C,
                const int N) {
    int idx = get_global_id(0);
    if (idx < N) {
        C[idx] = A[idx] + B[idx];
    }
}

// Host code in C for setting up and executing the kernel
// 1. Create an OpenCL context and command queue.
// 2. Allocate device memory buffers.
// 3. Copy data to device buffers.
// 4. Build the kernel program from source.
// 5. Set kernel arguments and enqueue the kernel for execution.
// 6. Read back the results and release resources.
```

Emerging Programming Paradigms

Beyond CUDA and OpenCL, new programming models and languages continue to evolve, such as:

- **SYCL:**
  A higher-level abstraction built on OpenCL that allows single-source programming in C++. It simplifies code development for heterogeneous systems by unifying host and device code.
- **Vulkan Compute:**
  Originally designed for graphics, Vulkan's compute capabilities are being explored for general-purpose GPU tasks, offering low-level access to GPU hardware with improved performance and flexibility.

These emerging paradigms strive to simplify parallel programming while providing robust performance across a variety of hardware platforms.

2.5 Simulation and Modeling Techniques in GPU Design

Simulation and modeling are critical tools for both GPU developers and researchers. They allow for performance analysis, architectural exploration, and design validation without the need for physical hardware prototypes. In this section, we discuss various tools and methods used to simulate GPU performance and behavior.

Tools for GPU Simulation

Several simulation tools have been developed to model GPU architectures accurately. These tools help in understanding the performance characteristics of GPU designs and in identifying potential bottlenecks.

- **GPGPU-Sim:**
  An open-source simulator that models the behavior of modern GPUs at a detailed architectural level. It is widely used in academic research to evaluate new architectural ideas and optimizations.

- **Multi2Sim:**
  A simulation framework that supports both CPU and GPU architectures, allowing for heterogeneous system simulation.
- **NVIDIA Nsight Systems and Nsight Compute:**
  While not traditional simulators, these tools provide detailed profiling and analysis of GPU applications, helping developers understand performance issues on actual hardware.

Modeling Techniques

Analytical Modeling

Analytical models are used to estimate GPU performance based on simplified mathematical representations of the hardware. They typically involve:

- **Queuing Theory:**
  Modeling the behavior of memory requests and execution pipelines as queues to predict latency and throughput.
- **Roofline Model:**
  A visual model that relates computational performance to memory bandwidth. The roofline model helps identify whether an application is compute-bound or memory-bound.

Cycle-Accurate Simulation

Cycle-accurate simulators emulate the GPU at the clock cycle level. These models are very detailed and provide insights into the exact timing of events within the GPU. However, they are computationally intensive and typically used in research rather than for everyday application development.

High-Level Modeling

High-level simulation frameworks abstract away the cycle-level details to provide faster, albeit less precise, estimates of GPU performance. These models are useful for:

- **Algorithm Development:**
  Quickly assessing the impact of different algorithmic choices on overall performance.

- **Architectural Exploration:**
  Evaluating the performance trade-offs of different design parameters (e.g., number of cores, memory sizes) without detailed hardware simulation.

Example: Using the Roofline Model

The roofline model is a common analytical tool used to understand the performance limits of a GPU. It is typically represented as a graph with:

- **X-Axis:**
  Operational intensity (flops per byte of memory accessed).
- **Y-Axis:**
  Achievable performance (in flops per second).

A simplified table summarizing a roofline analysis might look like this:

Parameter	Value	Description
Peak Compute Performance	10 TFLOPS	The maximum floating-point operations per second the GPU can perform.
Memory Bandwidth	500 GB/s	The rate at which data can be read from or written to memory.
Operational Intensity	2 FLOPS/byte	Ratio of computations to memory operations for the application.

Using these parameters, one can determine whether an application is limited by compute performance or by memory bandwidth, guiding optimization efforts.

Summary

In this chapter, we explored the core components of GPU architecture, including compute units, memory hierarchy, and interconnects, which together dictate the performance and efficiency of a GPU. We also introduced key GPU programming models—CUDA, OpenCL, and emerging paradigms like SYCL and Vulkan Compute—and provided practical code examples to illustrate how these models work in real applications. Finally, we examined various simulation and modeling techniques used to analyze and optimize GPU designs, from detailed cycle-accurate simulations to high-level analytical models such as the roofline model.

Chapter 3: Deep Dive into Advanced GPU Architectures

In this chapter, we delve into the advanced aspects of GPU design, exploring how modern architectures have evolved from simple, fixed-function pipelines into highly flexible and programmable systems. We will examine the evolution of GPU pipelines, the development of modern multi-core and heterogeneous designs, and the techniques used to optimize memory architecture and bandwidth for maximum throughput.

3.1 Evolution from Fixed Function Pipelines to Programmable Shaders

Fixed Function Pipelines

Fixed function pipelines were the cornerstone of early graphics processing. In these systems, each stage of the graphics pipeline—such as vertex processing, rasterization, and fragment processing—was hardwired to perform a specific set of operations. The advantages of this approach were simplicity and speed for standard operations like texture mapping, lighting, and color blending.

- **Advantages:**
    - **Optimized Performance:** Each stage was optimized for a particular task, ensuring high throughput for common rendering operations.
    - **Simplicity:** With fixed functionality, hardware design was straightforward and predictable.
- **Limitations:**
    - **Inflexibility:** The inability to modify pipeline stages meant that innovative effects or non-standard operations were difficult or impossible to implement.
    - **Limited Creativity:** Developers were confined to the capabilities built into the hardware, restricting the evolution of more complex visual effects.

The Shift to Programmable Shaders

The evolution of GPU architecture took a significant turn with the introduction of **programmable shaders**. This architectural shift allowed developers to write custom programs—commonly known as **vertex shaders**, **fragment (or pixel) shaders**, and later **geometry**, **tessellation**, and **compute shaders**—that could manipulate graphics data in highly flexible ways.

- **Key Developments:**
    - **Vertex Shaders:** Replaced fixed-function vertex processing, allowing dynamic manipulation of vertex data. This enabled more complex transformations and deformations of 3D models.
    - **Fragment Shaders:** Offered control over pixel-level operations, facilitating advanced effects such as per-pixel lighting, texture blending, and procedural texture generation.
    - **Geometry and Tessellation Shaders:** Introduced additional programmable stages that provided more control over geometry processing, including the ability to generate or refine geometric detail dynamically.
    - **Compute Shaders:** Extended the GPU's capabilities beyond graphics, enabling general-purpose parallel computations for tasks such as physics simulations, image processing, and deep learning.

Impact on Flexibility and Innovation

The introduction of programmable shaders transformed GPUs into versatile computing devices:

- **Enhanced Visual Effects:** Custom shader programs allow for the creation of sophisticated lighting models, dynamic shadows, and real-time post-processing effects.
- **Adaptability:** Developers can update and improve the visual quality of applications through software updates without requiring hardware changes.
- **Cross-Domain Applications:** The programmable nature of modern GPUs has opened the door for their use in fields beyond graphics, such as scientific computing and artificial intelligence, by enabling general-purpose parallel computing.

Summary Table: Fixed Function vs. Programmable Pipelines

Aspect	Fixed Function Pipeline	Programmable Shaders
Flexibility	Limited to predefined operations	Highly flexible, allowing custom algorithms
Customization	Minimal; developers work within hardware limits	Extensive; developers write custom shader code
Innovation Potential	Restricted by hardware capabilities	Enables continuous innovation and sophisticated effects
Application Scope	Primarily graphics rendering	Graphics rendering and general-purpose computing

3.2 Modern Multi-Core and Heterogeneous Designs

Multi-Core GPU Architectures

Modern GPUs are characterized by their **multi-core architectures**, featuring hundreds to thousands of smaller processing units (shader cores) grouped into larger blocks, such as Streaming Multiprocessors (SMs) or Compute Units (CUs).

- **Parallel Execution:**
    - **Massive Parallelism:** With a large number of cores working simultaneously, GPUs can process many threads at once, which is essential for handling data-parallel tasks.
    - **SIMT Execution Model:** GPUs use a Single Instruction, Multiple Threads (SIMT) model where a single instruction stream is executed across multiple cores. This model is highly efficient for workloads that can be divided into many small, similar operations.
- **Scalability:**
    - **Thread Blocks and Grids:** In programming frameworks like CUDA and OpenCL, threads are organized into blocks and grids, allowing the GPU to scale operations according to the problem size.
    - **Load Balancing:** Efficient scheduling and resource management within multi-core architectures ensure that all cores are effectively utilized, maximizing performance.

Heterogeneous Designs

Heterogeneous computing refers to systems that integrate different types of processing units—typically CPUs and GPUs—to capitalize on the strengths of each.

- **CPU-GPU Collaboration:**
  - **Complementary Roles:** CPUs handle complex, sequential tasks and system-level management, while GPUs excel at parallel data processing.
  - **Workload Offloading:** Tasks that are highly parallelizable, such as matrix multiplications or image processing, are offloaded to the GPU, freeing the CPU to manage control tasks and I/O operations.
- **Specialized Units:**
  - **Tensor Cores:** Found in some modern GPUs, tensor cores are dedicated to accelerating deep learning computations, providing significant performance gains for neural network training and inference.
  - **Ray Tracing Cores:** These cores are specialized for handling real-time ray tracing calculations, enabling realistic lighting, reflections, and shadows in graphics applications.

Interplay of Cores and Specialized Units

The combination of general-purpose cores and specialized hardware within a heterogeneous GPU architecture creates a balanced system capable of addressing diverse computational challenges.

- **Example Scenario:**
  In a modern game, the GPU might use:
  - **Shader Cores:** For processing vertex and pixel data.
  - **Tensor Cores:** To accelerate physics simulations or AI-driven elements within the game.
  - **Ray Tracing Cores:** To compute realistic lighting and reflections.

Diagram: Simplified Heterogeneous GPU Architecture

sql

```
+------------------------------------+
```

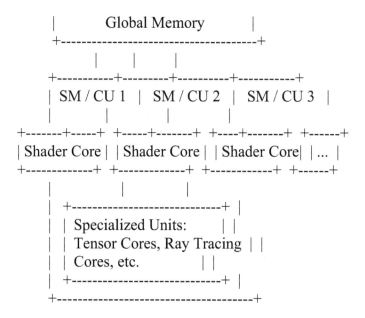

```
|        Global Memory        |
+-----------------------------------+
    |      |      |
+-----------+---------+----------+-----------+
| SM / CU 1  |  SM / CU 2  |  SM / CU 3  |
    |      |      |      |
+-------+-----+ +-----+-------+ +----+-------+ +------+
| Shader Core | | Shader Core | | Shader Core| | ... |
+-------------+ +-------------+ +------------+ +------+
    |        |        |
    |  +----------------------------+ |
    |  | Specialized Units:        | |
    |  | Tensor Cores, Ray Tracing  | |
    |  | Cores, etc.               | |
    |  +----------------------------+ |
    +-----------------------------------+
```

This diagram illustrates how general-purpose shader cores are complemented by specialized units, all working in concert to deliver high-performance computing across multiple domains.

3.3 Memory Architecture and Bandwidth Optimization

Importance of Memory Architecture

Memory architecture plays a critical role in overall GPU performance. Efficient management of data movement and storage directly affects computational throughput and latency. The following strategies are employed to maximize memory performance:

Techniques for Bandwidth Optimization

1. **Memory Coalescing:**
   o **Definition:** Memory coalescing refers to combining multiple memory accesses into a single, efficient operation.
   o **Impact:** When threads in a warp (or wavefront) access contiguous memory addresses, the hardware can merge these

requests, reducing the number of memory transactions and lowering latency.

- o **Example:**
  In CUDA, ensuring that threads access sequential elements of an array promotes coalescing. For instance, if thread i accesses element A[i], the hardware can merge these accesses if A is stored contiguously.

2. **Utilizing Shared Memory:**
   - o **Definition:** Shared memory is a small, fast on-chip memory that is accessible by all threads within a block.
   - o **Usage:** Frequently accessed data can be loaded into shared memory, significantly reducing the number of slower global memory accesses.
   - o **Implementation Tip:**
     In a CUDA kernel, using shared memory might look like this:

cpp

```cpp
__global__ void optimizedKernel(const float *input, float *output, int N) {
    extern __shared__ float sharedData[];
    int idx = threadIdx.x + blockIdx.x * blockDim.x;

    // Load data from global memory to shared memory
    if (idx < N) {
        sharedData[threadIdx.x] = input[idx];
    }
    __syncthreads(); // Ensure all threads have loaded data

    // Perform computation using shared data
    if (idx < N) {
        output[idx] = sharedData[threadIdx.x] * 2.0f; // Example computation
    }
}
```

Explanation:
This code snippet demonstrates how data is loaded from global memory into shared memory. The __syncthreads() call ensures all threads complete the load before proceeding, which minimizes access latency during computation.

3. **Effective Cache Utilization:**
   - **L1 and L2 Caches:**
     Modern GPUs include on-chip caches to speed up access to frequently used data. Optimizing data reuse patterns can improve cache hit rates, thus enhancing performance.
   - **Cache Blocking:**
     Organizing data into blocks that fit into the cache (cache blocking) can reduce cache misses. This technique is particularly effective in matrix operations where sub-blocks of the matrix are reused multiple times.
4. **Reducing Memory Contention:**
   - **Bank Conflicts:**
     When multiple threads attempt to access the same memory bank simultaneously, bank conflicts occur, leading to delays. Organizing data and access patterns to avoid conflicts is essential.
   - **Padding and Alignment:**
     Data structures may be padded or aligned in memory to ensure that concurrent accesses do not lead to conflicts. For instance, aligning arrays on boundaries that match the cache line size can improve efficiency.

Bandwidth Optimization Summary Table

Technique	Purpose	Benefit	Implementation Considerations
Memory Coalescing	Merge multiple accesses into fewer transactions	Reduced latency and higher throughput	Ensure contiguous memory access patterns
Shared Memory Usage	Store frequently used data on-chip	Faster access compared to global memory	Manage shared memory size and synchronize threads
Cache Utilization	Increase cache hit rates through data reuse	Faster data access through L1/L2 caches	Apply cache blocking techniques
Reducing Memory Contention	Avoid simultaneous access conflicts	Minimizes delays and improves parallelism	Use padding, alignment, and optimize access patterns

Summary

In this section, we examined the advanced aspects of GPU memory architecture and techniques to optimize bandwidth. By leveraging memory coalescing, shared memory, effective cache utilization, and careful management of memory contention, developers can significantly enhance the performance of GPU applications. These optimizations ensure that the high computational throughput of modern multi-core GPUs is not hampered by memory access delays.

Chapter 4: The Evolution of GPUs: Milestones and Technological Breakthroughs

The history of Graphics Processing Units (GPUs) is a fascinating journey marked by continuous innovation and transformative breakthroughs. This chapter provides a detailed chronology of key milestones in GPU development and examines how Moore's Law and advances in semiconductor technology have driven the evolution of these powerful devices.

4.1 Historical Milestones in GPU Development

Early Beginnings: The Birth of Graphics Accelerators

In the early days of personal computing, the central processing unit (CPU) was tasked with handling all computations, including graphics rendering. However, as graphical user interfaces (GUIs) and early video games became popular, the need for specialized hardware to manage graphical tasks emerged.

- **1980s: Emergence of 2D Graphics Accelerators**
  Early graphics accelerators were designed to handle 2D operations, such as drawing lines, shapes, and simple bitmapped images. These devices offloaded basic graphical tasks from the CPU, thereby improving performance in applications and early video games.

Transition to 3D Graphics

As software evolved, so did the demand for more realistic and dynamic visuals.

- **Early 1990s: Introduction of 3D Accelerators**
  With the rise of 3D video games and multimedia applications, dedicated 3D accelerators entered the market. Companies like ATI and NVIDIA began developing hardware capable of handling three-

dimensional rendering, which involved more complex operations such as texture mapping, shading, and depth buffering.

- **1999: The NVIDIA GeForce 256**
  Often cited as the world's first GPU, the GeForce 256 marked a significant leap in graphics processing. It introduced hardware-based transformation and lighting (T&L), which offloaded these tasks from the CPU and allowed for more sophisticated 3D graphics. This innovation laid the foundation for modern GPU architectures.

The Era of Programmable Shaders

The advent of programmable shaders revolutionized the GPU landscape by providing unprecedented flexibility in graphics processing.

- **Early 2000s: Programmable Shaders Become Mainstream**
  With the introduction of vertex and fragment shaders, developers could now write custom programs to control how vertices and pixels were processed. This shift from fixed-function pipelines to programmable pipelines enabled the creation of more realistic lighting, shadows, and complex visual effects.
- **2006 Onwards: General-Purpose GPU Computing (GPGPU)**
  Technologies like NVIDIA's CUDA platform expanded the role of GPUs beyond graphics. By leveraging their massive parallelism, GPUs began to be used for scientific simulations, data analysis, and machine learning. This era marked the beginning of GPUs being recognized as essential compute engines across diverse fields.

Recent Milestones and Breakthroughs

- **2010s: The Rise of Deep Learning and AI**
  The surge in deep learning research demanded rapid training of large neural networks. GPUs, with their parallel processing capabilities, became the hardware of choice for training complex models, accelerating breakthroughs in artificial intelligence.
- **Late 2010s to Early 2020s: Advanced Architectures and Specialized Units**
  Modern GPUs now include specialized cores—such as tensor cores for deep learning and ray tracing cores for realistic graphics—to optimize performance for specific applications. These advancements have pushed the boundaries of what is possible in both gaming and professional computing.

Timeline of Key Milestones

Below is a timeline summarizing some of the most significant milestones in GPU development:

Year/Decade	Milestone	Description
1980s	Early 2D Graphics Accelerators	Hardware dedicated to basic 2D rendering, offloading simple graphics tasks from the CPU.
Early 1990s	Introduction of 3D Accelerators	Emergence of hardware capable of 3D rendering, paving the way for more immersive graphics.
1999	NVIDIA GeForce 256	First GPU with hardware-based T&L, marking a turning point in graphics performance.
Early 2000s	Programmable Shaders Introduced	Shift from fixed-function to programmable pipelines, enabling custom visual effects.
2006	CUDA and GPGPU	NVIDIA launches CUDA, opening the door for GPUs to be used in general-purpose computing.
2010s	Rise of Deep Learning	GPUs become central to training deep neural networks, fueling advances in AI.
Late 2010s – 2020s	Advanced Architectures (Tensor and Ray Tracing Cores)	Modern GPUs incorporate specialized units to enhance performance in AI and realistic rendering.

4.2 The Impact of Moore's Law and Semiconductor Advances

Moore's Law: The Engine of Innovation

Moore's Law is the observation that the number of transistors on a microchip doubles approximately every two years, while the cost of computers is halved. Although originally an empirical observation, Moore's

Law has served as a guiding principle for semiconductor development for decades.

- **Transistor Density and Performance:**
  As transistor densities increase, GPUs can pack more processing cores into the same chip area, boosting parallelism and overall computational power. This exponential growth has allowed GPUs to evolve from handling simple graphics tasks to executing complex computations in parallel.
- **Cost and Efficiency:**
  Advances driven by Moore's Law have not only increased performance but also reduced the cost per transistor. This reduction has made it economically feasible to produce high-performance GPUs for both consumer and professional markets.

Semiconductor Advances: Materials and Manufacturing Innovations

The evolution of semiconductor technology has played a crucial role in GPU advancement. Several key innovations have contributed to the modern GPU landscape:

1. **Lithography Improvements:**
   - **Smaller Process Nodes:**
     The transition from larger to smaller process nodes (e.g., from 90nm to 7nm and beyond) has enabled manufacturers to increase transistor density, improve power efficiency, and boost clock speeds.
   - **Extreme Ultraviolet (EUV) Lithography:**
     EUV lithography has allowed for even finer feature sizes, further pushing the boundaries of transistor scaling.
2. **New Materials and Transistor Designs:**
   - **FinFET Technology:**
     FinFET (Fin Field-Effect Transistor) designs offer improved control over current flow, reducing leakage and enhancing performance. This technology has been widely adopted in modern GPUs to achieve better energy efficiency and higher performance.
   - **Advanced Dielectric Materials:**
     Innovations in materials science, including the development of high-κ (high-kappa) dielectrics, have improved transistor performance by allowing for better insulation and reduced power consumption.

44

3. **3D Integration and Packaging:**
   - **3D Stacking:**
     Modern GPUs sometimes employ 3D stacking techniques, where multiple layers of transistors are built on top of each other. This approach increases density without expanding the chip's footprint.
   - **Advanced Interconnects:**
     Technologies such as NVLink and PCI Express 4.0/5.0 provide high-bandwidth connections between GPUs and other system components, ensuring that the increased processing power is effectively utilized.

The Synergy Between Moore's Law and GPU Evolution

The relentless pace of semiconductor innovation has enabled GPUs to keep pace with, and often exceed, the performance improvements predicted by Moore's Law. This synergy has led to:

- **Exponential Growth in Compute Power:**
  Increased transistor densities and improved manufacturing techniques have allowed GPUs to deliver performance leaps with each new generation.
- **Enhanced Energy Efficiency:**
  As process nodes shrink and transistor designs evolve, GPUs are not only faster but also more energy efficient, which is critical for applications ranging from mobile devices to large-scale data centers.
- **Broadening Application Domains:**
  The combination of Moore's Law and semiconductor advances has expanded the role of GPUs beyond graphics, making them indispensable in fields such as artificial intelligence, scientific research, and high-performance computing.

Summary Table: Impact of Semiconductor Advances

Aspect	Advancement	Impact on GPUs
Process Node Shrinking	Transition from larger to smaller nodes (e.g., 90nm → 7nm)	Higher transistor density, improved performance, and better energy efficiency
Lithography	Adoption of EUV lithography	Finer feature sizes, enabling more complex and powerful chip designs

Aspect	Advancement	Impact on GPUs
Transistor Technology	Introduction of FinFET and high-κ dielectrics	Reduced leakage, higher performance, and increased power efficiency
3D Integration	Use of 3D stacking and advanced packaging techniques	Increased density without expanding chip size; improved interconnect speeds
Interconnect Technology	Development of NVLink, PCIe 4.0/5.0	High-bandwidth communication between GPUs and other system components

4.3 Innovations in Chip Manufacturing

The rapid evolution of GPU performance is not solely a result of architectural breakthroughs—it is also driven by innovations in chip manufacturing. Advances in lithography, packaging, and 3D integration techniques have been instrumental in pushing the limits of what GPUs can achieve. This section explores these key innovations and explains how they contribute to enhanced performance, energy efficiency, and overall capability.

Lithography

Lithography is the process used to transfer circuit patterns onto a semiconductor wafer. It is a critical step in chip manufacturing because the resolution and precision of lithography directly affect the density of transistors on a chip.

- **Process Node Shrinking:**
  As lithography techniques improve, manufacturers are able to reduce the process node (e.g., from 90nm to 7nm and beyond). This reduction allows more transistors to be packed into the same physical space, which in turn increases the computational power and efficiency of GPUs.
- **Extreme Ultraviolet (EUV) Lithography:**
  EUV lithography uses light with a very short wavelength (around 13.5 nm) to create finer details on chips. This advanced technique

enables the production of chips with even smaller features, which are essential for modern GPUs that require high transistor densities.

- o **Impact:**
  EUV lithography not only improves performance by increasing transistor count but also helps reduce power consumption since smaller transistors can operate at lower voltages.

Packaging Techniques

Packaging refers to how a semiconductor chip is enclosed and connected to the external environment, including other chips and system components.

- **Traditional Packaging:**
  In conventional packaging, the chip is mounted on a substrate that facilitates electrical connections and heat dissipation. As GPUs have grown more complex, traditional packaging methods have evolved to handle increased heat output and high-speed data transfer.
- **Advanced Packaging Solutions:**
  Innovations such as flip-chip technology and interposer-based designs have emerged to improve thermal performance and signal integrity.
  - o **Flip-Chip Technology:**
    In flip-chip packaging, the chip is mounted upside down, allowing for shorter electrical paths between the chip and the substrate. This results in reduced signal delay and improved power efficiency.
  - o **Interposers:**
    An interposer is a layer that sits between the chip and the package, providing additional routing for electrical signals. This technique is particularly useful in multi-chip modules and high-bandwidth applications.

3D Integration Techniques

3D integration is a groundbreaking approach that involves stacking multiple layers of semiconductor devices vertically rather than spreading them out horizontally on a single silicon die.

- **3D Stacking:**
  In 3D stacking, several layers of active circuitry are fabricated and then bonded together. This method allows for significantly higher transistor densities without increasing the chip's footprint.
- **Through-Silicon Vias (TSVs):**
  TSVs are vertical electrical connections that pass through the silicon layers, providing fast and efficient communication between stacked chips.
  - **Advantages:**
    TSVs reduce the distance that electrical signals need to travel, leading to lower latency and higher bandwidth. They also enable tighter integration of different functional units, which is essential for heterogeneous computing systems.
- **Impact on GPUs:**
  By employing 3D integration, GPU manufacturers can build more powerful and energy-efficient devices. Increased transistor density and improved interconnect performance directly translate to better computational throughput and faster memory access.

Summary Table: Innovations in Chip Manufacturing

Innovation	Description	Key Benefits
Lithography	Advanced photolithography (e.g., EUV) for creating fine circuit details.	Higher transistor density, lower power consumption, improved performance.
Advanced Packaging	Techniques like flip-chip and interposers for better heat dissipation and signal integrity.	Reduced signal delays, enhanced thermal management, and increased reliability.
3D Integration	Stacking multiple layers of semiconductor devices using TSVs.	Greater transistor density, faster inter-layer communication, and improved overall efficiency.

4.4 AI's Influence on GPU Evolution

The rise of artificial intelligence (AI) and machine learning (ML) has had a profound impact on GPU development. As AI applications require enormous amounts of parallel computation, GPU architectures have evolved to meet these new demands. This section examines how AI has reshaped GPU design and the resulting innovations.

Driving Forces from AI

- **Massive Parallel Processing Needs:**
  Training deep neural networks involves a vast number of matrix and vector operations that can be processed in parallel. GPUs, with their thousands of cores, are naturally suited for these tasks.
- **Demand for Specialized Hardware:**
  AI workloads have spurred the creation of specialized hardware units within GPUs. For example:
  - **Tensor Cores:**
    Tensor cores are specialized units designed to accelerate the types of matrix multiplications and convolutions that are common in deep learning. They allow for significant speedups in training and inference by performing multiple calculations simultaneously.
  - **Enhanced Memory Architectures:**
    AI applications often involve processing large datasets, requiring high memory bandwidth and efficient data movement. Innovations such as high-bandwidth memory (HBM) and improved caching strategies have been developed to meet these needs.

Architectural Changes Driven by AI

- **Programmability and Flexibility:**
  Modern GPUs are designed to be highly programmable, allowing researchers and developers to implement custom algorithms optimized for AI workloads. This flexibility has been key in adapting GPUs to the rapidly changing landscape of AI research.

- **Integration of AI Frameworks:**
  Software ecosystems around GPUs have evolved to include AI-specific libraries and frameworks. NVIDIA's CUDA, for example, has been complemented by cuDNN (a deep neural network library) and TensorRT (a high-performance deep learning inference optimizer). These tools simplify the process of deploying AI models on GPUs.
- **Scalability for Data Centers:**
  As AI applications scale, there is an increasing demand for GPUs that can operate efficiently in data centers. Newer GPU architectures are designed with scalability in mind, ensuring that they can be integrated into large computing clusters for tasks such as real-time inference and high-throughput training.

AI's Role in Future GPU Innovations

- **Continued Architectural Refinements:**
  The ongoing requirements of AI will likely drive further refinements in GPU architecture. We can expect to see even more specialized cores, enhanced interconnects, and improved energy efficiency as AI workloads become more complex.
- **Synergy Between AI and GPU Research:**
  The relationship between AI and GPU development is mutually beneficial. Advances in AI algorithms often push the boundaries of hardware performance, while improvements in GPU technology enable researchers to experiment with more sophisticated models and larger datasets.
- **Emerging Technologies:**
  Future GPU designs may incorporate emerging technologies such as neuromorphic computing and quantum accelerators, which are inspired by the way the human brain processes information. These innovations could further accelerate AI performance and open new avenues for research.

Summary Table: AI's Influence on GPU Evolution

Aspect	Impact of AI	Resulting Innovations
Parallel Processing	High demand for simultaneous computations in neural networks.	Increased core counts and specialized units (e.g., tensor cores).
Memory Bandwidth	Large datasets require rapid data movement.	Adoption of high-bandwidth memory (HBM) and improved caching.
Programmability	Need for flexible hardware to support evolving AI models.	Development of programmable shaders and integration with AI libraries.
Scalability	AI applications demand efficient data center operations.	Architectures optimized for cluster environments and data centers.

4.5 Trends and Roadmaps for the Next Generation of GPUs

The evolution of GPU technology is a dynamic and ongoing process, driven by both market demands and rapid advances in semiconductor technology. In this section, we explore the emerging trends and anticipated roadmaps that are set to shape the next generation of GPUs from a technological perspective.

Emerging Architectural Trends

Increased Core Counts and Heterogeneity

- **Expansion of Parallelism:**
  Future GPUs are expected to continue the trend of increasing core counts, enabling even greater parallel processing capabilities. This increase will further enhance performance for data-parallel tasks such as deep learning and scientific simulations.
- **Heterogeneous Architectures:**
  The next generation of GPUs will likely integrate a broader mix of specialized cores, such as enhanced tensor cores, dedicated ray tracing units, and possibly new units designed specifically for AI

workloads or even emerging fields like quantum-inspired computing. These heterogeneous architectures are designed to provide tailored processing for a variety of tasks, reducing latency and increasing overall efficiency.

Enhanced Memory Technologies

- **Next-Generation High-Bandwidth Memory (HBM):**
  Advances in memory technology will continue to improve the bandwidth available to GPUs. Future generations are expected to utilize newer versions of HBM or similar technologies, increasing the rate at which data can be transferred and processed.
- **On-Chip Memory Innovations:**
  Innovations in cache design and shared memory organization will further reduce latency. Techniques such as adaptive caching and intelligent prefetching are likely to be incorporated to enhance data reuse and minimize memory bottlenecks.

Improved Interconnects and Scalability

- **Faster Interconnect Technologies:**
  Technologies like PCIe 5.0/6.0 and NVLink are expected to be further refined, providing even higher data transfer rates between GPUs and other system components. These improvements are critical for scaling performance in multi-GPU configurations and data center environments.
- **Scalable Multi-GPU Architectures:**
  Future GPUs will feature improved scalability, with enhanced communication protocols between multiple GPUs in a system. This will facilitate larger, more complex computing clusters, ideal for both AI training and high-performance computing (HPC) applications.

Power Efficiency and Thermal Innovations

- **Optimized Power Management:**
  With increasing core counts and higher performance, managing power consumption remains a key challenge. Future GPUs are likely to incorporate more advanced dynamic voltage and frequency scaling (DVFS), power gating, and clock gating techniques to maintain energy efficiency.
- **Advanced Cooling Solutions:**
  As GPUs become more powerful, innovative cooling solutions—

including improved liquid cooling systems, advanced heat dissipation materials, and integrated thermal management designs—will be crucial to ensure that performance gains do not come at the expense of reliability or lifespan.

Anticipated Roadmaps

Short-Term Roadmap (Next 1-2 Years)

- **Incremental Improvements:**
  The immediate future will likely see iterative improvements in existing architectures. Manufacturers are expected to release GPUs that offer higher performance through refined process nodes, enhanced memory subsystems, and optimized power management.
- **Software Ecosystem Enhancements:**
  In parallel, software tools, drivers, and AI libraries will continue to evolve, providing developers with more efficient ways to harness GPU capabilities. Expect tighter integration with frameworks like TensorFlow, PyTorch, and industry-specific solutions.

Mid-Term Roadmap (2-5 Years)

- **Introduction of New Architectures:**
  Over the next few years, major GPU vendors are expected to unveil entirely new architectures that incorporate significant advancements in heterogeneous design, including more robust AI accelerators and dedicated cores for emerging workloads.
- **Focus on Data Center and Cloud Integration:**
  As AI and HPC demands grow, GPUs will be designed with enhanced scalability and multi-GPU configurations to serve data centers and cloud computing environments more effectively.
- **Adoption of Next-Gen Memory Technologies:**
  Wider adoption of next-generation HBM or equivalent high-speed memory solutions is anticipated, delivering significant boosts in overall throughput and reducing latency in data-intensive applications.

Long-Term Roadmap (Beyond 5 Years)

- **Revolutionary Processing Paradigms:**
  In the longer term, we may witness the advent of GPUs that integrate fundamentally new processing paradigms. These could include neuromorphic computing architectures inspired by the human brain, or quantum-accelerated co-processors that work in tandem with classical GPUs.
- **Full Convergence of Heterogeneous Computing:**
  The boundaries between CPU, GPU, and other specialized processors are expected to blur further, leading to a unified processing model where tasks are seamlessly distributed across the most efficient hardware unit, regardless of its traditional classification.

Summary Table: Roadmap for Next-Generation GPUs

Roadmap Stage	Key Developments	Expected Impact
Short-Term (1-2 Years)	Incremental performance gains, enhanced software ecosystems	Improved efficiency and better integration in existing applications.
Mid-Term (2-5 Years)	New architectures with enhanced heterogeneity, advanced memory, scalability	Significant performance boosts in AI, HPC, and data center deployments.
Long-Term (Beyond 5 Years)	Revolutionary processing paradigms, full convergence of heterogeneous computing	Potential paradigm shifts in computing, with seamless task distribution across diverse processing units.

4.6 Convergence of Graphics, Compute, and AI

The traditional boundaries separating graphics processing, general-purpose computation, and artificial intelligence are increasingly converging. This convergence is driven by both technological innovation and the evolving needs of modern applications.

Blurring the Lines

Unified Architectures

- **Multi-Purpose Cores:**
  Modern GPUs are no longer solely dedicated to rendering graphics. With the integration of programmable shaders, tensor cores, and other specialized units, the same hardware is used for graphics rendering, scientific computing, and AI training. This unified architecture enables more efficient use of resources and simplifies the development process.
- **Software Integration:**
  Contemporary software frameworks support multiple domains on a single hardware platform. For example, APIs such as Vulkan and DirectX 12 allow developers to manage both graphics and compute tasks, while AI libraries integrate seamlessly with these APIs to leverage GPU acceleration for neural network training.

Benefits of Convergence

- **Improved Performance and Efficiency:**
  The convergence of graphics, compute, and AI enables the sharing of resources across different workloads. A unified GPU can dynamically allocate processing power where it is needed most, leading to better overall system performance and efficiency.
- **Simplified Development:**
  Developers benefit from a single, integrated platform that supports diverse applications. This reduces the complexity of managing separate hardware for graphics and computation, allowing for more streamlined software development and easier cross-domain innovation.
- **Innovation in User Experiences:**
  The blending of graphics and AI is driving new applications in virtual reality (VR), augmented reality (AR), and mixed reality. For instance, real-time AI-driven image enhancement and dynamic scene rendering are becoming possible due to the unified processing power of modern GPUs.

Real-World Applications

Example: Real-Time Ray Tracing with AI Enhancements

- **Graphics Rendering:**
  Modern GPUs use ray tracing cores to compute realistic lighting and shadows in real time. This technique simulates the way light interacts with objects, resulting in highly realistic images.
- **AI Integration:**
  At the same time, AI algorithms can be employed to upscale lower-resolution images or denoise rendered frames, further enhancing visual quality. This integration allows for smoother, more immersive experiences in gaming and virtual environments.
- **Unified Workflow:**
  The same GPU handles both the computationally intensive ray tracing calculations and the AI-based post-processing, showcasing the benefits of converged architectures.

Code Example: Simplified Shader Incorporating AI-Based Denoising

Below is a simplified pseudocode example illustrating how a graphics shader might integrate an AI-based denoising algorithm within a rendering pipeline:

cpp

```
// Pseudocode for a shader that applies ray tracing and AI-based denoising

// Ray tracing function (simplified)
vec3 traceRay(Ray ray) {
    // Compute intersections and lighting (simplified logic)
    vec3 color = computeLighting(ray);
    return color;
}

// AI-based denoising function (simplified)
vec3 denoise(vec3 color, vec3 neighboringColors[9]) {
    // Apply a simple weighted average for denoising
    vec3 sum = color;
    for (int i = 0; i < 9; i++) {
        sum += neighboringColors[i];
    }
    return sum / 10.0;
}

// Main shader function
void main() {
```

```
Ray ray = generateRayForPixel();
vec3 tracedColor = traceRay(ray);

// Sample neighboring pixels (simplified)
vec3 neighbors[9] = sampleNeighboringPixels();

// Apply AI-based denoising
vec3 finalColor = denoise(tracedColor, neighbors);

outputColor = finalColor;
}
```

Explanation:

- The shader first performs ray tracing to compute the color for a pixel.
- It then samples neighboring pixel colors, which could be used by an AI-based denoising algorithm.
- Finally, a denoising function is applied to smooth out noise and improve image quality, demonstrating the convergence of graphics rendering and AI processing.

Convergence Trends Summary Table

Domain	Traditional Focus	Converged Approach	Benefits
Graphics	Real-time rendering, fixed-function pipelines	Programmable shaders, ray tracing cores integrated with AI processing	Enhanced realism, real-time effects, and improved visual quality
Compute	General-purpose parallel computations	Unified cores serving both graphics and compute workloads	Efficient resource sharing, simplified development
AI	Dedicated neural network processing	Specialized AI accelerators (e.g., tensor cores) within GPU architecture	Accelerated AI training and inference, enhanced application performance

Chapter Summary

In this section of Chapter 4, we examined the forward-looking trends and roadmaps that signal the next generation of GPU technology. We discussed how emerging architectural trends, enhanced memory and interconnect technologies, and advanced power and thermal management strategies will drive future GPU performance. We also explored the convergence of graphics, compute, and AI—highlighting how modern GPU architectures are unifying these domains to deliver unprecedented performance, efficiency, and versatility.

Chapter 5: Cutting-Edge Applications in Gaming

Modern gaming is undergoing a revolutionary transformation, powered largely by advanced GPU architectures. In this chapter, we explore how cutting-edge GPUs are enabling next-generation gaming engines to deliver immersive, lifelike experiences and how real-time ray tracing and advanced rendering techniques are transforming visual quality in games.

5.1 GPUs in Next-Generation Gaming Engines

Overview

Next-generation gaming engines harness the extraordinary parallel processing power of modern GPUs to create immersive worlds and dynamic environments. These engines use advanced architectural features—such as programmable shaders, high-speed memory, and specialized cores—to deliver realistic graphics, fluid animations, and interactive gameplay.

Key Architectural Enhancements in Gaming GPUs

1. **Massive Parallelism:**
   - **Description:**
     Modern GPUs contain thousands of cores that work in parallel. This allows them to handle millions of graphical operations simultaneously, such as transforming vertices, shading pixels, and processing physics.
   - **Impact on Gaming:**
     High levels of parallelism mean that complex scenes with numerous objects, dynamic lighting, and particle effects can be rendered smoothly and in real time.
2. **Programmable Shaders:**
   - **Description:**
     Programmable shaders replace fixed-function pipelines with custom code that can be tailored for specific visual effects. Vertex shaders, pixel (or fragment) shaders, and geometry shaders allow developers to implement complex visual algorithms.

- o **Impact on Gaming:**
  Custom shaders enable more realistic character animations, dynamic shadows, and special effects that adapt to gameplay conditions.

3. **Advanced Memory and Data Throughput:**
   - o **Description:**
     With high-bandwidth memory (such as GDDR6 or HBM) and improved memory hierarchies, modern GPUs minimize latency and maximize data throughput.
   - o **Impact on Gaming:**
     Faster memory access means that large textures, high-resolution models, and real-time physics data can be processed without lag, leading to smoother gameplay and more detailed environments.

4. **Specialized Hardware Units:**
   - o **Description:**
     Modern GPUs often include dedicated units such as tensor cores (for AI tasks) and ray tracing cores (for realistic lighting).
   - o **Impact on Gaming:**
     These specialized units offload specific tasks from the general-purpose cores, allowing for real-time enhancements in visual fidelity and game mechanics.

Practical Examples in Gaming Engines

Example: Real-Time Physics Simulation

Modern gaming engines use GPU acceleration for real-time physics simulations. Consider a game that simulates fluid dynamics—such as water, smoke, or explosions. These simulations involve solving complex equations in parallel across many data points. GPUs can accelerate these computations by processing thousands of simulation elements concurrently.

Simplified Pseudocode for GPU-Accelerated Physics Simulation (CUDA-like):

cpp

```
// CUDA kernel for a basic physics update on a set of particles
__global__ void updatePhysics(Particle *particles, int numParticles, float deltaTime) {
```

```
int idx = blockIdx.x * blockDim.x + threadIdx.x;
if (idx < numParticles) {
    // Update position based on velocity
    particles[idx].position += particles[idx].velocity * deltaTime;
    // Apply gravity
    particles[idx].velocity.y -= 9.81f * deltaTime;
    // Simple collision check with ground (y=0)
    if (particles[idx].position.y < 0) {
        particles[idx].position.y = 0;
        particles[idx].velocity.y *= -0.5f; // Dampen the bounce
    }
}
}
```

Explanation:

- The kernel updatePhysics computes the new position and velocity for each particle in parallel.
- Each GPU thread updates one particle, ensuring that thousands of particles can be simulated simultaneously.
- This parallelism is essential for delivering smooth, realistic physics effects in complex gaming environments.

Integration into Gaming Engines

Next-generation engines such as Unreal Engine 5 and Unity 202X integrate these GPU advancements to deliver features like:

- **Dynamic Lighting and Shadows:**
  Utilizing programmable shaders and ray tracing cores to create realistic, time-of-day-specific lighting effects.
- **Enhanced Realism:**
  Using advanced material and texture mapping techniques to simulate surfaces, reflections, and refractions.
- **Interactive Environments:**
  Enabling real-time physics and AI-driven interactions that respond dynamically to player inputs.

5.2 Real-Time Ray Tracing and Advanced Rendering Techniques

Overview

Real-time ray tracing is a breakthrough technology that simulates the way light interacts with objects to create stunningly realistic images. Unlike traditional rasterization techniques that approximate lighting and shadows, ray tracing calculates the path of individual light rays for each pixel, producing lifelike reflections, refractions, and shadows.

Fundamentals of Ray Tracing

- **Ray Casting:**
  - **Description:**
    Ray tracing begins by casting rays from the camera into the scene. Each ray is used to determine what objects it intersects.
  - **Impact:**
    This method provides accurate visibility information, which is fundamental for creating realistic images.
- **Lighting and Shading Calculations:**
  - **Description:**
    After a ray intersects an object, further rays are cast to simulate the effects of light sources. These secondary rays help determine the intensity, color, and shadows at the point of intersection.
  - **Impact:**
    This results in more accurate simulations of soft shadows, reflections, and refractions.

Hardware Acceleration for Ray Tracing

Modern GPUs incorporate specialized hardware—often known as **ray tracing cores**—to accelerate these computations:

- **Dedicated Ray Tracing Cores:**
  These cores are optimized for calculating intersections and managing the complex data structures needed for ray tracing.
- **Hybrid Rendering Pipelines:**
  Many current systems use a hybrid approach, where traditional

rasterization handles most of the scene while ray tracing is applied selectively to enhance visual effects.

Advanced Rendering Techniques

Real-Time Ray Tracing in Gaming

Real-time ray tracing is used in gaming to enhance realism without compromising performance:

- **Dynamic Reflections:**
  Accurately simulating reflective surfaces (e.g., water, glass, polished metal) in real time.
- **Soft Shadows:**
  Producing natural, soft-edged shadows that vary in intensity based on the light source and distance.
- **Global Illumination:**
  Simulating the indirect lighting that results from light bouncing off surfaces, creating more natural and vibrant scenes.

Example: Simplified Shader for Ray Tracing

Below is a simplified pseudocode example of a shader function that performs basic ray tracing and incorporates advanced rendering techniques:

cpp

```
// Pseudocode for a simplified ray tracing shader function

// Function to trace a ray and compute the color at the intersection
vec3 traceRay(Ray ray, Scene scene) {
    Intersection hit = scene.findIntersection(ray);
    if (hit.exists) {
        // Calculate local lighting at the hit point
        vec3 localColor = computeLocalIllumination(hit, scene);
        // Cast a secondary ray for reflections (if the material is reflective)
        if (hit.material.reflectivity > 0.0) {
            Ray reflectionRay = computeReflectionRay(ray, hit.normal);
            vec3 reflectedColor = traceRay(reflectionRay, scene);
            // Combine local color with reflected color
            return mix(localColor, reflectedColor, hit.material.reflectivity);
        }
```

```
    return localColor;
  }
  // Return background color if no intersection is found
  return scene.backgroundColor;
}

// Main shader function to compute the final color for a pixel
void main() {
  Ray primaryRay = generatePrimaryRay();
  vec3 finalColor = traceRay(primaryRay, scene);
  outputColor = finalColor;
}
```

Explanation:

- **traceRay Function:**
  - The function simulates the process of ray tracing by finding the first intersection of a ray with objects in the scene.
  - It computes local illumination based on the materials and light sources present.
  - If the material is reflective, it recursively casts a reflection ray and blends the results using the material's reflectivity parameter.
- **main Function:**
  - The primary ray is generated from the camera perspective.
  - The final color for each pixel is determined by tracing this primary ray, incorporating both direct lighting and reflections.
- This pseudocode illustrates the basic principles of ray tracing and how advanced techniques can be integrated into a shader to achieve lifelike graphics.

Benefits of Advanced Rendering Techniques

- **Visual Realism:**
  Real-time ray tracing creates scenes that are closer to reality by accurately simulating the behavior of light.
- **Immersive Experiences:**
  Enhanced lighting, shadows, and reflections contribute to more immersive gaming experiences, drawing players deeper into virtual worlds.
- **Dynamic Environments:**
  These techniques enable environments that respond naturally to

changes in lighting and player interactions, adding to the overall realism and excitement of the game.

5.3 Virtual Reality (VR) and Augmented Reality (AR) Innovations

Virtual Reality (VR) and Augmented Reality (AR) represent the next frontier in interactive entertainment and immersive computing. Both technologies rely heavily on advanced GPU capabilities to render complex, high-resolution scenes in real time while maintaining low latency—a critical requirement for user comfort and immersion.

The Role of GPUs in VR and AR

Real-Time Rendering and Low Latency

- **High Frame Rates:**
  To deliver smooth, immersive experiences in VR and AR, GPUs must render scenes at very high frame rates (typically 90 frames per second or higher). This minimizes motion sickness and enhances the feeling of presence.
- **Low Latency:**
  Latency—the delay between user movement and the corresponding update on the display—must be minimized. GPUs achieve this by processing vast amounts of data in parallel and optimizing the rendering pipeline to deliver near-instantaneous visual feedback.

High-Resolution and Stereoscopic Displays

- **Stereoscopic Rendering:**
  VR systems typically require two separate images (one for each eye) to create a stereoscopic 3D effect. This effectively doubles the rendering workload, making efficient GPU performance critical.
- **High-Resolution Textures and Models:**
  For immersive realism, VR and AR applications often use high-resolution textures and complex 3D models. Advanced GPUs with large amounts of high-bandwidth memory can handle these requirements without compromising on speed.

Enhanced Interactive Environments

- **Dynamic Scene Adjustments:**
  GPUs can dynamically adjust scene parameters—such as lighting, shading, and reflections—in real time based on user interactions. This responsiveness is essential for maintaining the realism and interactivity of VR and AR environments.
- **Sensor Integration and Environment Mapping:**
  Modern VR/AR systems integrate data from various sensors (e.g., head tracking, hand controllers) and use GPU-accelerated algorithms to adjust the displayed scene accordingly. Techniques such as environment mapping and real-time ray tracing can further enhance realism.

Innovations in VR and AR Rendering Techniques

Foveated Rendering

- **Concept:**
  Foveated rendering is a technique that leverages the human visual system's focus on the center of the field of view. The GPU renders the central area in high resolution while using lower resolution for the peripheral regions.
- **Benefits:**
  This approach significantly reduces the computational load without noticeable loss of visual quality, allowing for improved performance and power efficiency.

Asynchronous Timewarp and Spacewarp

- **Description:**
  Asynchronous timewarp (ATW) and spacewarp (ASW) are techniques used to compensate for latency. They work by reprojecting already rendered frames based on the latest head-tracking data.
- **Impact:**
  These techniques help maintain a seamless and stable visual experience even if there are minor delays in rendering, enhancing user comfort in VR environments.

Practical Example: Basic VR Rendering Pipeline (Pseudocode)

Below is a simplified pseudocode example demonstrating a basic VR rendering pipeline that handles stereoscopic rendering:

cpp

```cpp
// Pseudocode for VR rendering using two separate viewports for
stereoscopic display

// Function to render a scene from a given eye's perspective
void renderSceneForEye(Eye eye, Camera camera, Scene scene) {
    // Adjust the camera parameters based on the eye (left or right)
    Camera eyeCamera = adjustCameraForEye(camera, eye);

    // Set the viewport for the current eye
    setViewport(eye);

    // Clear the framebuffer
    clearFramebuffer();

    // Render the scene using the adjusted camera
    for (Object obj : scene.objects) {
        // Render each object using the eye-specific camera parameters
        renderObject(obj, eyeCamera);
    }
}

// Main rendering loop for VR
void renderVRFrame(Camera mainCamera, Scene scene) {
    // Render the scene for the left eye
    renderSceneForEye(LEFT_EYE, mainCamera, scene);

    // Render the scene for the right eye
    renderSceneForEye(RIGHT_EYE, mainCamera, scene);

    // Apply asynchronous timewarp to compensate for any latency
    applyAsynchronousTimewarp();

    // Present the final stereoscopic frame to the VR display
    presentFrame();
}
```

Explanation:

- **Camera Adjustment:**
  The adjustCameraForEye function adjusts the main camera's position and orientation for the left or right eye to create a stereoscopic effect.
- **Viewport Setting:**
  The setViewport function defines the area on the screen where each eye's image will be rendered.
- **Asynchronous Timewarp:**
  The applyAsynchronousTimewarp function is used to reproject rendered frames based on updated head-tracking data, reducing latency.
- **Frame Presentation:**
  Finally, the presentFrame function sends the composite stereoscopic image to the VR headset.

5.4 Graphics Optimization and Performance Tuning

Balancing visual fidelity and performance is a critical challenge in modern gaming and interactive applications. Graphics optimization and performance tuning ensure that games run smoothly while delivering high-quality visuals. This section delves into various techniques and strategies to achieve that perfect balance.

Key Areas for Optimization

1. Shader Optimization

- **Efficient Shader Code:**
  Writing optimized shader code is crucial. Avoiding complex mathematical operations when possible, reusing computed values, and minimizing conditional branches can reduce processing overhead.
- **Precomputation and Caching:**
  Precomputing frequently used values and storing them in constant memory or registers can reduce redundant computations during shader execution.

2. Level of Detail (LOD) Techniques

- **Dynamic LOD:**
  Level of Detail techniques adjust the complexity of 3D models based on their distance from the camera. Distant objects can be rendered with fewer polygons, reducing the GPU load without a noticeable impact on visual quality.
- **Texture LOD:**
  Similar to geometric LOD, texture LOD uses lower-resolution textures for distant objects. Mipmapping is a common technique where precomputed, downscaled versions of a texture are used based on the object's distance from the camera.

3. Memory Access Optimization

- **Memory Coalescing:**
  Ensure that threads in a warp access contiguous memory locations to enable memory coalescing, which reduces the number of memory transactions and increases throughput.
- **Shared Memory Utilization:**
  Frequently accessed data can be stored in shared memory to reduce global memory latency. As shown in previous examples, effective use of shared memory can lead to significant performance improvements.

4. Rendering Pipeline Optimization

- **Culling Techniques:**
  Implement view frustum culling, occlusion culling, and backface culling to avoid rendering objects that are not visible to the camera. This reduces the number of draw calls and the overall rendering workload.
- **Batching and Instancing:**
  Combining similar objects into a single draw call (batching) or using instancing to draw multiple copies of the same object efficiently can drastically reduce CPU overhead and improve rendering speed.

5. Profiling and Tuning

- **Performance Profilers:**
  Use tools such as NVIDIA Nsight, AMD Radeon GPU Profiler, or Intel Graphics Performance Analyzers to profile your application.

These tools help identify bottlenecks in the rendering pipeline, such as shader inefficiencies, memory bandwidth issues, or excessive draw calls.

- **Iterative Tuning:**
  Optimization is an iterative process. Regularly profile your application, identify bottlenecks, apply optimizations, and then re-profile to ensure that performance improvements are realized.

Practical Example: Optimizing a Shader

Consider a fragment shader that applies a lighting effect. Below is a simplified example of an optimized shader compared to a less optimized version.

Less Optimized Shader (Pseudocode):

glsl

```
// Less optimized fragment shader pseudocode
void main() {
    vec3 normal = normalize(cross(dFdx(position), dFdy(position)));
    vec3 lightDir = normalize(lightPosition - position);
    float diffuse = max(dot(normal, lightDir), 0.0);
    vec3 diffuseColor = diffuse * lightColor;

    // Complex conditional for ambient lighting
    vec3 ambientColor;
    if (diffuse < 0.5) {
        ambientColor = vec3(0.2, 0.2, 0.2);
    } else {
        ambientColor = vec3(0.1, 0.1, 0.1);
    }

    vec3 finalColor = diffuseColor + ambientColor;
    gl_FragColor = vec4(finalColor, 1.0);
}
```

Optimized Shader (Pseudocode):

glsl

```
// Optimized fragment shader pseudocode
```

```
void main() {
    // Precompute normal using built-in functions for efficiency
    vec3 normal = normalize(cross(dFdx(position), dFdy(position)));
    vec3 lightDir = normalize(lightPosition - position);
    float diffuse = max(dot(normal, lightDir), 0.0);

    // Use a smoothstep function to blend ambient lighting instead of
conditionals
    float ambientFactor = smoothstep(0.0, 1.0, diffuse);
    vec3 ambientColor = mix(vec3(0.2), vec3(0.1), ambientFactor);

    vec3 finalColor = (diffuse * lightColor) + ambientColor;
    gl_FragColor = vec4(finalColor, 1.0);
}
```

Explanation:

- **Precomputation:**
  The optimized shader reuses computed values, avoiding redundant calculations.
- **Conditional Replacement:**
  Instead of a conditional statement, the optimized version uses the smoothstep function to blend ambient lighting smoothly. This reduces branching, which is particularly beneficial in a parallel execution environment.
- **Result:**
  These optimizations lead to a shader that executes faster on the GPU while delivering similar visual quality.

Summary Table: Graphics Optimization Techniques

Technique	Purpose	Key Benefits
Shader Optimization	Streamline shader code and reduce complexity	Lower execution time, reduced computational overhead
Level of Detail (LOD)	Adjust complexity based on object distance	Reduced polygon count, improved rendering speed
Memory Access Optimization	Enhance memory throughput (coalescing, shared memory)	Faster data access, lower latency

Technique	Purpose	Key Benefits
Culling and Batching	Reduce unnecessary rendering	Fewer draw calls, reduced CPU overhead
Profiling and Tuning	Identify and address performance bottlenecks	Iterative improvements leading to better overall performance

5.5 Industry Case Studies: GPU-Driven Gaming Platforms

In this section, we examine real-world examples from leading game developers and hardware manufacturers that highlight how GPU-driven platforms are transforming the gaming landscape. These case studies demonstrate the impact of advanced GPU architectures on the creation of immersive experiences, high-fidelity graphics, and responsive gameplay.

Case Study 1: NVIDIA GeForce and Game Development

Overview

NVIDIA's GeForce series has been a driving force in the evolution of PC gaming. With each new generation, NVIDIA has pushed the boundaries of graphical performance and introduced features that have set new industry standards.

Key Innovations

- **Ray Tracing and DLSS:**
  NVIDIA's RTX series introduced real-time ray tracing and Deep Learning Super Sampling (DLSS).
  - *Ray Tracing:* Uses dedicated RT cores to simulate realistic lighting, reflections, and shadows, significantly enhancing visual realism in games.
  - *DLSS:* Leverages AI to upscale lower-resolution images to higher resolutions without sacrificing performance, ensuring smooth gameplay even at high resolutions.
- **Software Ecosystem:**
  The GeForce Experience software provides game optimization

settings, driver updates, and additional features such as ShadowPlay for game recording. This ecosystem simplifies the process of maintaining peak performance and visual quality.

Example: "Cyberpunk 2077"

- **Technical Demands:**
  "Cyberpunk 2077" is known for its highly detailed open-world environment, dynamic weather effects, and complex lighting scenarios. The game benefits immensely from NVIDIA's RTX technology, which allows for real-time ray-traced reflections and shadows.
- **Performance Impact:**
  With GPUs like the RTX 3080, players experience high frame rates at 4K resolution, making the game not only visually stunning but also playable on high-end systems.

Case Study 2: AMD Radeon and Cross-Platform Gaming

Overview

AMD's Radeon GPUs have long been favored for their excellent price-to-performance ratio and open ecosystem support. AMD's focus on open standards, such as Vulkan and DirectX 12, has made their GPUs popular among game developers and a wide range of gaming platforms.

Key Innovations

- **High Bandwidth Memory (HBM):**
  AMD has pioneered the use of HBM in its GPUs, which provides higher memory bandwidth and improved energy efficiency. This technology is especially important for rendering complex scenes with large textures and detailed models.
- **Optimized Multi-Platform Support:**
  AMD's emphasis on open standards ensures that its GPUs deliver consistent performance across different platforms—from high-end PCs to gaming consoles like the PlayStation 5 and Xbox Series X.

Example: "Assassin's Creed Valhalla"

- **Technical Demands:**
  "Assassin's Creed Valhalla" features expansive, detailed open-world environments and realistic character models. The game benefits from AMD's efficient memory management and optimized graphics pipelines.
- **Performance Impact:**
  On systems powered by AMD's Radeon RX 6000 series, the game achieves high frame rates with stable performance, providing a smooth gaming experience even in graphically intensive scenarios.

Case Study 3: Integrated GPU Solutions in Gaming Laptops

Overview

Gaming laptops have become increasingly popular due to advancements in mobile GPU technology. Manufacturers are now able to pack powerful GPUs into portable systems without compromising performance.

Key Innovations

- **Optimized Thermal and Power Management:**
  Mobile GPUs are engineered with advanced cooling systems and power management features that allow them to run at high performance in a compact form factor.
- **Hybrid Graphics Solutions:**
  Many gaming laptops employ hybrid graphics, combining an integrated GPU with a dedicated mobile GPU. This setup enables dynamic switching between power-saving modes and high-performance modes based on the task.

Example: "Call of Duty: Warzone"

- **Technical Demands:**
  "Call of Duty: Warzone" requires high frame rates and low latency for competitive play, even on the move.
- **Performance Impact:**
  Gaming laptops equipped with NVIDIA's GeForce RTX mobile GPUs deliver smooth, responsive gameplay with high-quality visuals,

proving that advanced GPU technology can meet the demands of competitive, portable gaming.

Summary Table: Industry Case Studies Overview

Case Study	GPU Platform	Key Innovations	Representative Game/Application
NVIDIA GeForce	RTX Series	Real-time ray tracing, DLSS, robust software ecosystem	Cyberpunk 2077
AMD Radeon	RX 6000 Series	High Bandwidth Memory (HBM), cross-platform support, open standards	Assassin's Creed Valhalla
Integrated GPU Solutions (Laptops)	GeForce RTX Mobile, Hybrid Solutions	Optimized thermal/power management, hybrid graphics	Call of Duty: Warzone

5.6 The Future of Gaming: Cloud Gaming and Beyond

The future of gaming is rapidly evolving with the emergence of cloud gaming and other innovative paradigms. These trends are redefining how games are developed, distributed, and experienced by players around the world.

Cloud Gaming: A Paradigm Shift

Overview

Cloud gaming leverages powerful data centers and high-speed internet to stream games directly to users on various devices, including PCs, smartphones, and smart TVs. Rather than relying on local hardware, the heavy computational work is done in remote servers equipped with high-end GPUs.

Key Advantages

- **Accessibility:**
  Cloud gaming enables users to play high-quality games without investing in expensive hardware. Even devices with modest specifications can stream games rendered on powerful servers.
- **Instant Play:**
  With cloud gaming, games can be played instantly without lengthy downloads or installations. This model also supports cross-platform play, allowing gamers to access their titles on multiple devices.
- **Scalability:**
  Game developers can optimize their titles for high-performance GPUs in data centers, ensuring consistent quality and performance regardless of the end-user's hardware.

Leading Cloud Gaming Platforms

- **NVIDIA GeForce Now:**
  Leverages NVIDIA's powerful GPUs to deliver high-quality streaming with features like RTX-enabled ray tracing for enhanced graphics.
- **Google Stadia:**
  Offers a subscription-based service that streams games from Google's data centers, promising high resolution and low latency.
- **Microsoft xCloud:**
  Part of the Xbox ecosystem, xCloud allows gamers to stream titles from Xbox Game Pass, utilizing Microsoft's Azure cloud infrastructure.

Practical Example: Streaming a High-Fidelity Game

Imagine playing a graphically intensive game like "Control" on a mid-range laptop. The cloud gaming platform handles all the complex rendering and physics computations using high-end GPUs in a data center. The final output is streamed over the internet to your device, delivering a smooth, high-resolution gaming experience.

Beyond Cloud Gaming: Emerging Trends

Mobile and Edge Computing

- **5G Connectivity:**
  The widespread adoption of 5G networks will significantly reduce latency, making mobile gaming and cloud gaming even more viable. Gamers will enjoy seamless streaming experiences, even on the go.
- **Edge Computing:**
  By deploying smaller data centers closer to end users, edge computing minimizes latency further and improves the responsiveness of cloud gaming services.

Virtual and Augmented Reality in the Cloud

- **Remote VR/AR Experiences:**
  Cloud gaming is set to expand into VR and AR, enabling users to experience immersive environments without the need for bulky local hardware. Remote servers equipped with high-end GPUs can render VR/AR content in real time and stream it with minimal latency.
- **Collaborative and Social Gaming:**
  Cloud platforms can facilitate multi-user VR and AR experiences, opening up new possibilities for social interaction and collaborative gameplay in virtual worlds.

AI-Enhanced Gaming Experiences

- **Adaptive Graphics and Real-Time Optimization:**
  Future gaming platforms will increasingly integrate AI to dynamically adjust graphical settings and optimize performance based on real-time data. This can lead to personalized gaming experiences that adapt to both the game's demands and the player's preferences.
- **Content Generation:**
  AI-driven tools are beginning to assist in content creation, from procedural level design to character animations, further blurring the line between developer-driven and player-driven content.

Summary Table: The Future of Gaming

Trend	Description	Key Benefits
Cloud Gaming	Streaming high-fidelity games from remote servers with powerful GPUs.	Increased accessibility, instant play, reduced hardware costs.
5G and Edge Computing	Faster networks and localized data centers to reduce latency.	Improved responsiveness, seamless mobile gaming.
VR/AR in the Cloud	Cloud-rendered virtual and augmented reality experiences.	High-quality immersive experiences without local hardware constraints.
AI-Enhanced Gaming	Integration of AI for adaptive graphics, real-time optimization, and content generation.	Personalized experiences, enhanced visuals, streamlined development.

Chapter Summary

In Chapter 5, we explored how advanced GPUs are revolutionizing the gaming industry through cutting-edge applications. In section 5.5, we examined industry case studies that highlighted the pivotal roles played by NVIDIA GeForce, AMD Radeon, and integrated GPU solutions in driving immersive, high-performance gaming platforms. Real-world examples, such as "Cyberpunk 2077," "Assassin's Creed Valhalla," and "Call of Duty: Warzone," showcased the tangible benefits of advanced GPU technology in modern gaming.

Chapter 6: Cutting-Edge Applications in Machine Learning and AI

The rise of machine learning (ML) and artificial intelligence (AI) has been profoundly accelerated by the capabilities of modern GPUs. Their ability to perform thousands of parallel operations simultaneously makes them the preferred hardware for training and deploying complex deep learning models. In this chapter, we will explore how GPU acceleration enhances deep learning, and we will examine popular GPU-optimized ML frameworks that have revolutionized the way researchers and developers build intelligent systems.

6.1 GPU Acceleration in Deep Learning: An Overview

Why GPUs Are the Preferred Choice for Training Complex Models

Massive Parallelism and Throughput

- **Parallel Computation:**
  GPUs consist of thousands of smaller cores that can operate simultaneously. This architecture is ideal for the matrix and vector operations that dominate deep learning workloads, where many calculations must be performed concurrently.
- **High Throughput:**
  The ability of GPUs to process large blocks of data in parallel leads to significantly higher throughput compared to traditional CPUs. In deep learning, where datasets can be massive and models extremely complex, this high throughput translates to faster training times and quicker iterations.

Efficiency in Handling Data-Intensive Operations

- **Optimized for Matrix Operations:**
  Deep learning involves many linear algebra operations (e.g., matrix multiplications, convolutions) that are computationally intensive. GPUs are specifically designed to handle these operations efficiently, thanks to their highly parallelized architecture.
- **Reduced Training Time:**
  By offloading compute-intensive tasks to the GPU, training times for deep neural networks can be reduced from weeks to days—or even hours. This efficiency accelerates research and development cycles, enabling rapid experimentation and innovation.

Specialized Hardware and Software Ecosystem

- **Dedicated Tensor Cores:**
  Recent GPU architectures, such as NVIDIA's Volta, Turing, and Ampere, feature tensor cores. These specialized units are designed specifically for the high-speed processing of tensor operations, which are fundamental in deep learning. Tensor cores can deliver orders-of-magnitude performance improvements for tasks like convolution and matrix multiplication.
- **Robust Software Support:**
  GPU vendors provide comprehensive software libraries and development tools that simplify the integration of GPU acceleration into machine learning workflows. Examples include NVIDIA's CUDA platform and cuDNN (CUDA Deep Neural Network library), which are widely used to optimize deep learning frameworks.

Practical Example: Matrix Multiplication on a GPU

Matrix multiplication is a common operation in deep learning. Consider multiplying two large matrices AAA and BBB to produce a matrix CCC:

cpp

```cpp
// CUDA Kernel for simple matrix multiplication
__global__ void matrixMulKernel(float* A, float* B, float* C,
int N) {
    int row = blockIdx.y * blockDim.y + threadIdx.y;
    int col = blockIdx.x * blockDim.x + threadIdx.x;

    if (row < N && col < N) {
        float value = 0;
```

```
        for (int k = 0; k < N; k++) {
            value += A[row * N + k] * B[k * N + col];
        }
        C[row * N + col] = value;
    }
}

int main() {
    int N = 1024; // Assume a 1024x1024 matrix
    size_t size = N * N * sizeof(float);

    // Allocate memory on host
    float* h_A = (float*)malloc(size);
    float* h_B = (float*)malloc(size);
    float* h_C = (float*)malloc(size);

    // Initialize matrices h_A and h_B (omitted for brevity)

    // Allocate memory on device
    float *d_A, *d_B, *d_C;
    cudaMalloc(&d_A, size);
    cudaMalloc(&d_B, size);
    cudaMalloc(&d_C, size);

    // Copy matrices from host to device
    cudaMemcpy(d_A, h_A, size, cudaMemcpyHostToDevice);
    cudaMemcpy(d_B, h_B, size, cudaMemcpyHostToDevice);

    // Define grid and block dimensions
    dim3 threadsPerBlock(16, 16);
    dim3 blocksPerGrid((N + threadsPerBlock.x - 1) /
threadsPerBlock.x,
                       (N + threadsPerBlock.y - 1) /
threadsPerBlock.y);

    // Launch the kernel
    matrixMulKernel<<<blocksPerGrid, threadsPerBlock>>>(d_A,
d_B, d_C, N);

    // Copy result back to host
    cudaMemcpy(h_C, d_C, size, cudaMemcpyDeviceToHost);

    // Clean up device memory
    cudaFree(d_A);
    cudaFree(d_B);
    cudaFree(d_C);

    // Free host memory
    free(h_A);
    free(h_B);
    free(h_C);
```

```
    return 0;
}
```

Explanation:

- The CUDA kernel `matrixMulKernel` performs matrix multiplication in parallel by dividing the matrices into blocks and threads.
- Each thread computes one element of the result matrix CCC by iterating through a row of AAA and a column of BBB.
- This parallel execution significantly reduces the computation time compared to a serial CPU implementation.

Summary Table: Benefits of GPU Acceleration in Deep Learning

Feature	Description	Impact on Deep Learning
Massive Parallelism	Thousands of cores operate simultaneously	Faster processing of large datasets and complex models
High Throughput	Optimized for parallel data operations	Reduced training times and faster iteration cycles
Specialized Hardware (Tensor Cores)	Dedicated units for tensor operations	Significant performance gains in convolution and matrix multiplications
Robust Software Ecosystem	Libraries like CUDA and cuDNN support GPU integration	Simplifies development and maximizes hardware utilization

6.2 Exploring GPU-Optimized ML Frameworks

Modern machine learning frameworks have been optimized to leverage the computational power of GPUs. In this section, we will look at some of the most popular frameworks—TensorFlow, PyTorch, and others—detailing how they use GPUs to accelerate deep learning tasks.

TensorFlow

Overview

- **Developed by:**
  Google Brain Team
- **Key Features:**
  - **Graph-Based Computation:**
    TensorFlow represents computations as dataflow graphs, where nodes represent operations and edges represent the data (tensors) flowing between them.
  - **GPU Support:**
    TensorFlow can seamlessly offload operations to GPUs, optimizing performance for both training and inference.
  - **Wide Ecosystem:**
    Extensive libraries and tools such as TensorBoard for visualization and TensorFlow Lite for mobile deployment.

Code Example: Training a Simple Neural Network in TensorFlow

Below is a simplified example of training a neural network on the MNIST dataset using TensorFlow with GPU support:

```python
import tensorflow as tf
from tensorflow.keras import layers, models

# Check if GPU is available
print("GPU available:",
tf.config.list_physical_devices('GPU'))

# Load and preprocess the MNIST dataset
mnist = tf.keras.datasets.mnist
(x_train, y_train), (x_test, y_test) = mnist.load_data()
x_train, x_test = x_train / 255.0, x_test / 255.0

# Define a simple neural network model
model = models.Sequential([
    layers.Flatten(input_shape=(28, 28)),
    layers.Dense(128, activation='relu'),
    layers.Dropout(0.2),
    layers.Dense(10, activation='softmax')
])

# Compile the model
model.compile(optimizer='adam',
              loss='sparse_categorical_crossentropy',
              metrics=['accuracy'])
```

```
# Train the model (GPU acceleration is used automatically if
available)
model.fit(x_train, y_train, epochs=5, batch_size=64)

# Evaluate the model
test_loss, test_acc = model.evaluate(x_test, y_test)
print("Test accuracy:", test_acc)
```

Explanation:

- **GPU Detection:**
  The code first checks if a GPU is available.
- **Data Preprocessing:**
  The MNIST dataset is loaded and normalized.
- **Model Definition:**
  A simple sequential neural network is defined using Keras layers.
- **Training:**
  The model is trained using the Adam optimizer, with TensorFlow
  automatically leveraging the GPU to accelerate computations.

PyTorch

Overview

- **Developed by:**
  Facebook's AI Research lab (FAIR)
- **Key Features:**
  - **Dynamic Computation Graphs:**
    PyTorch uses dynamic computation graphs (define-by-run),
    which provide greater flexibility and ease of debugging.
  - **GPU Acceleration:**
    PyTorch allows seamless transfer of tensors between CPU
    and GPU, making it straightforward to accelerate model
    training.
  - **Strong Community Support:**
    PyTorch has gained popularity for its ease of use and robust
    community contributions.

Code Example: Training a Neural Network in PyTorch

Below is a simplified example of training a neural network on the MNIST
dataset using PyTorch with GPU acceleration:

```python
import torch
import torch.nn as nn
import torch.optim as optim
from torchvision import datasets, transforms

# Check if GPU is available and set device
device = torch.device("cuda" if torch.cuda.is_available()
else "cpu")
print("Using device:", device)

# Define transformations and load the MNIST dataset
transform = transforms.Compose([transforms.ToTensor(),
transforms.Normalize((0.5,), (0.5,))])
train_dataset = datasets.MNIST(root='./data', train=True,
download=True, transform=transform)
train_loader = torch.utils.data.DataLoader(train_dataset,
batch_size=64, shuffle=True)

# Define a simple neural network model
class SimpleNN(nn.Module):
    def __init__(self):
        super(SimpleNN, self).__init__()
        self.flatten = nn.Flatten()
        self.fc1 = nn.Linear(28*28, 128)
        self.relu = nn.ReLU()
        self.dropout = nn.Dropout(0.2)
        self.fc2 = nn.Linear(128, 10)

    def forward(self, x):
        x = self.flatten(x)
        x = self.fc1(x)
        x = self.relu(x)
        x = self.dropout(x)
        x = self.fc2(x)
        return x

model = SimpleNN().to(device)

# Define loss function and optimizer
criterion = nn.CrossEntropyLoss()
optimizer = optim.Adam(model.parameters(), lr=0.001)

# Training loop
epochs = 5
for epoch in range(epochs):
    for batch_idx, (data, target) in enumerate(train_loader):
        data, target = data.to(device), target.to(device)
        optimizer.zero_grad()
        output = model(data)
```

```
        loss = criterion(output, target)
        loss.backward()
        optimizer.step()

    print(f'Epoch {epoch+1}/{epochs}, Loss:
{loss.item():.4f}')

# Note: Evaluation code would follow a similar pattern by
moving test data to the GPU.
```

Explanation:

- **Device Configuration:**
  The code first checks for GPU availability and sets the computation device accordingly.
- **Data Loading and Transformation:**
  The MNIST dataset is loaded with basic transformations and normalization.
- **Model Definition:**
  A simple neural network is defined using PyTorch's `nn.Module` and moved to the GPU using `.to(device)`.
- **Training Loop:**
  The model is trained over multiple epochs with loss computed on GPU-accelerated tensors.

Other Frameworks

- **MXNet, Chainer, and JAX:**
  While TensorFlow and PyTorch dominate the landscape, other frameworks like MXNet, Chainer, and JAX also offer robust GPU support. They provide unique features and optimizations that may suit specific research or production needs.

Summary Table: Comparison of GPU-Optimized ML Frameworks

Framework	Key Features	Programming Style	Popular Use Cases
TensorFlow	Graph-based computation,	Declarative (static graphs)	Production-grade applications, research,

Framework	Key Features	Programming Style	Popular Use Cases
	extensive ecosystem, TensorBoard		mobile/embedded devices
PyTorch	Dynamic computation graphs, ease of debugging, strong community support	Imperative (define-by-run)	Rapid prototyping, research, academic projects
Other Frameworks	Varying levels of abstraction and optimization techniques	Varies (often similar to above)	Specialized applications, high-performance computing

6.3 Parallel Processing for Neural Network Architectures

Deep neural networks, whether they are Convolutional Neural Networks (CNNs) for image processing, Recurrent Neural Networks (RNNs) for sequential data, or more advanced architectures like Transformers, rely on massive amounts of matrix and tensor operations. GPUs, with their inherent parallel processing capabilities, are exceptionally well-suited to accelerate these operations. In this section, we explore strategies for leveraging GPU parallelism in neural network architectures.

Strategies for Leveraging GPU Parallelism

1. Data Parallelism

Concept:
Data parallelism involves splitting the input data across multiple GPU cores so that the same operations (such as convolution or matrix multiplication) are applied concurrently on different parts of the data.

- **Implementation:**
  In a CNN, for example, each GPU thread or group of threads can

process a subset of image patches. During training, data is often divided into mini-batches that are processed in parallel.

- **Example Use Case:**
  If you have a mini-batch of 256 images and a GPU with thousands of cores, the workload can be distributed such that each core processes a few pixels or image patches concurrently.

2. Model Parallelism

Concept:
Model parallelism involves splitting a neural network model across multiple GPU cores. This approach is useful when the model is too large to fit into the memory of a single GPU.

- **Implementation:**
  Different layers or parts of a layer (such as different filters in a convolutional layer) can be assigned to different GPUs or different groups of cores within a GPU.
- **Challenges:**
  Model parallelism requires careful coordination and communication between the GPUs or cores to ensure that intermediate outputs are correctly transferred and aggregated.

3. Pipeline Parallelism

Concept:
Pipeline parallelism divides the neural network into sequential stages (or pipelines) that can be processed in parallel. Each pipeline stage is assigned to different GPU cores.

- **Implementation:**
  For instance, in a deep CNN, the first few layers can be processed by one group of cores, while subsequent layers are processed by another group. As soon as the first group finishes processing a mini-batch, the next group can start processing that output, creating a pipeline.
- **Benefits:**
  This method helps to keep all parts of the GPU busy and can reduce idle times, although it introduces some latency due to inter-stage communication.

4. Leveraging Specialized Hardware Units

Modern GPUs often include specialized cores—such as tensor cores (optimized for mixed-precision matrix operations)—which can be utilized to speed up key computations in deep learning.

- **Tensor Cores in CNNs:**
  These cores are particularly effective for the convolution operations common in CNNs, enabling a significant boost in throughput and efficiency.
- **Mixed-Precision Training:**
  By using a combination of single-precision (FP32) and half-precision (FP16) arithmetic, GPUs can increase computation speed while maintaining acceptable levels of model accuracy.

Practical Example: Parallel Convolution in a CNN

Below is a simplified pseudocode example that outlines how a convolution operation can be parallelized on a GPU using CUDA-like syntax:

cpp

```
// CUDA kernel for a 2D convolution operation on a single
input channel
__global__ void conv2dKernel(const float *input, const float
*kernel, float *output,
                            int inputWidth, int inputHeight,
int kernelWidth, int kernelHeight) {
    int x = blockIdx.x * blockDim.x + threadIdx.x;
    int y = blockIdx.y * blockDim.y + threadIdx.y;

    int kernelRadiusX = kernelWidth / 2;
    int kernelRadiusY = kernelHeight / 2;

    if (x < inputWidth && y < inputHeight) {
        float sum = 0.0f;
        // Iterate over the kernel
        for (int ky = -kernelRadiusY; ky <= kernelRadiusY;
ky++) {
            for (int kx = -kernelRadiusX; kx <=
kernelRadiusX; kx++) {
                int ix = min(max(x + kx, 0), inputWidth - 1);
                int iy = min(max(y + ky, 0), inputHeight -
1);
                float value = input[iy * inputWidth + ix];
                float weight = kernel[(ky + kernelRadiusY) *
kernelWidth + (kx + kernelRadiusX)];
                sum += value * weight;
            }
```

```
        }
        output[y * inputWidth + x] = sum;
    }
}

int main() {
    // Assume input dimensions and allocate memory for input,
kernel, and output
    int inputWidth = 1024, inputHeight = 1024;
    int kernelWidth = 3, kernelHeight = 3;
    size_t inputSize = inputWidth * inputHeight *
sizeof(float);
    size_t kernelSize = kernelWidth * kernelHeight *
sizeof(float);

    // Host allocations (omitted initialization code for
brevity)
    float *h_input, *h_kernel, *h_output;

    // Device allocations
    float *d_input, *d_kernel, *d_output;
    cudaMalloc(&d_input, inputSize);
    cudaMalloc(&d_kernel, kernelSize);
    cudaMalloc(&d_output, inputSize);

    // Copy data from host to device
    cudaMemcpy(d_input, h_input, inputSize,
cudaMemcpyHostToDevice);
    cudaMemcpy(d_kernel, h_kernel, kernelSize,
cudaMemcpyHostToDevice);

    // Define grid and block dimensions
    dim3 threadsPerBlock(16, 16);
    dim3 blocksPerGrid((inputWidth + threadsPerBlock.x - 1) /
threadsPerBlock.x,
                       (inputHeight + threadsPerBlock.y - 1)
/ threadsPerBlock.y);

    // Launch the convolution kernel
    conv2dKernel<<<blocksPerGrid, threadsPerBlock>>>(d_input,
d_kernel, d_output,

inputWidth, inputHeight,

kernelWidth, kernelHeight);

    // Copy the output back to host and clean up device
memory
    cudaMemcpy(h_output, d_output, inputSize,
cudaMemcpyDeviceToHost);
    cudaFree(d_input);
```

```
    cudaFree(d_kernel);
    cudaFree(d_output);

    return 0;
}
```

Explanation:

- The `conv2dKernel` function performs a 2D convolution over an image, where each thread computes the convolution for one pixel.
- Threads are organized in a two-dimensional grid corresponding to the image dimensions, ensuring that the convolution operation is performed in parallel across the entire image.
- This example demonstrates data parallelism—each thread works independently on different parts of the input data.

Summary Table: Parallel Processing Strategies for Neural Networks

Strategy	Description	Benefits
Data Parallelism	Splitting data into mini-batches processed concurrently by multiple cores	Faster processing, reduced training time
Model Parallelism	Dividing a large model across multiple GPUs or cores	Enables training of very large models
Pipeline Parallelism	Dividing the network into sequential stages processed in parallel	Improved utilization of GPU resources
Specialized Hardware	Utilizing tensor cores and mixed-precision arithmetic	Significant speedup for matrix and tensor operations

6.4 Case Studies: Breakthroughs in Computer Vision, NLP, and Reinforcement Learning

In this section, we explore real-world examples of how GPU acceleration has driven breakthroughs in various subfields of machine learning, including computer vision, natural language processing (NLP), and reinforcement learning. These case studies illustrate the transformative impact of GPU-enabled innovations.

Case Study 1: Computer Vision

Application: Image Classification and Object Detection

- **Example:**
  ResNet (Residual Networks) has become a foundational model in image classification. GPUs have allowed researchers to train deep ResNet models with hundreds of layers, enabling near-human accuracy on datasets like ImageNet.
- **GPU Role:**
  The massive parallelism of GPUs accelerates convolution operations and backpropagation, significantly reducing training time.
- **Real-World Impact:**
  Improved image recognition capabilities have led to advancements in autonomous vehicles, medical imaging, and security systems.

Code Example: Training ResNet with PyTorch

Below is a simplified code snippet demonstrating how a ResNet model is trained on the ImageNet dataset using PyTorch with GPU acceleration:

```python
python

import torch
import torch.nn as nn
import torch.optim as optim
import torchvision
import torchvision.transforms as transforms
from torchvision.models import resnet50

# Check for GPU availability
device = torch.device("cuda" if torch.cuda.is_available()
else "cpu")
print("Using device:", device)

# Data preprocessing and loading for ImageNet (simplified for
illustration)
transform = transforms.Compose([
    transforms.Resize(256),
    transforms.CenterCrop(224),
    transforms.ToTensor(),
```

```python
    transforms.Normalize(mean=[0.485, 0.456, 0.406],
std=[0.229, 0.224, 0.225])
])
# Assume ImageNet dataset is available in './imagenet_data'
train_dataset =
torchvision.datasets.ImageFolder(root='./imagenet_data/train'
, transform=transform)
train_loader = torch.utils.data.DataLoader(train_dataset,
batch_size=64, shuffle=True, num_workers=4)

# Load a pre-defined ResNet-50 model and move it to the GPU
model = resnet50(pretrained=False).to(device)

# Define loss function and optimizer
criterion = nn.CrossEntropyLoss()
optimizer = optim.SGD(model.parameters(), lr=0.01,
momentum=0.9)

# Training loop (simplified)
num_epochs = 5
for epoch in range(num_epochs):
    model.train()
    running_loss = 0.0
    for inputs, labels in train_loader:
        inputs, labels = inputs.to(device), labels.to(device)

        optimizer.zero_grad()
        outputs = model(inputs)
        loss = criterion(outputs, labels)
        loss.backward()
        optimizer.step()

        running_loss += loss.item()
    print(f"Epoch {epoch+1}/{num_epochs}, Loss:
{running_loss/len(train_loader):.4f}")

print("Training complete.")
```

Explanation:

- The code sets up a ResNet-50 model using PyTorch and trains it on a subset of the ImageNet dataset.
- GPU acceleration is leveraged by moving the model and data to the device specified by `torch.device("cuda")`.
- This setup dramatically reduces training time compared to CPU-based training.

Case Study 2: Natural Language Processing (NLP)

Application: Language Modeling and Machine Translation

- **Example:**
  Transformer-based models like BERT and GPT have revolutionized NLP by enabling unprecedented performance in language understanding and generation.
- **GPU Role:**
  GPUs accelerate the training of these models by handling the massive amounts of matrix multiplications involved in self-attention mechanisms.
- **Real-World Impact:**
  Breakthroughs in NLP have led to improved machine translation, sentiment analysis, and chatbots, enhancing user interactions with digital services.

Case Study 3: Reinforcement Learning

Application: Training Agents in Complex Environments

- **Example:**
  Deep Q-Networks (DQN) and **Proximal Policy Optimization (PPO)** have been successfully applied to train agents that learn to play video games or perform complex tasks.
- **GPU Role:**
  GPUs accelerate the simulation of environments and the computation of gradients during the training of reinforcement learning agents.
- **Real-World Impact:**
  These advancements have been applied to robotics, autonomous driving, and strategic game-playing AI, such as in the case of AlphaGo and OpenAI Five.

Summary Table: Case Studies in GPU-Accelerated Innovations

Field	Application	Model/Technique	GPU Contribution
Computer Vision	Image Classification, Object Detection	ResNet, YOLO, Mask R-CNN	Accelerated convolution, reduced training time
Natural Language Processing (NLP)	Language Modeling, Machine Translation	Transformers (BERT, GPT)	Efficient self-attention, rapid gradient computations
Reinforcement Learning	Training Agents in Complex Environments	DQN, PPO, Actor-Critic methods	Accelerated environment simulation, efficient policy updates

6.5 Overcoming Challenges in GPU-Driven AI

While GPUs have revolutionized the field of AI by significantly reducing training times and enabling the development of complex models, several challenges can impede optimal performance. In this section, we discuss common pitfalls encountered in GPU-driven AI workflows and outline strategies for overcoming these issues.

Common Pitfalls in GPU-Driven AI

1. Data Transfer Overhead

- **Issue:**
  Transferring data between the host (CPU) and the GPU can be time-consuming and may create a bottleneck if not managed properly.
- **Optimization Strategies:**
  - **Asynchronous Data Transfer:** Use asynchronous data transfers (e.g., CUDA streams) to overlap computation with data movement.

- o **Pinned Memory:** Allocate pinned (page-locked) memory on the host to speed up data transfers.
- o **Data Preprocessing on GPU:** Where possible, perform data preprocessing steps directly on the GPU to reduce the frequency of host-to-device transfers.

2. Memory Limitations and Management

- **Issue:**
  GPUs have limited memory compared to CPUs, which can become a constraint when training large models or using high-resolution data.
- **Optimization Strategies:**
  - o **Memory-Efficient Data Structures:** Use lower precision (e.g., FP16 or mixed precision) to reduce memory usage while maintaining model accuracy.
  - o **Gradient Checkpointing:** Save memory during training by recomputing intermediate activations on the fly rather than storing all of them.
  - o **Model and Data Parallelism:** Distribute the model or the data across multiple GPUs to manage memory usage more effectively.

3. Kernel Inefficiencies and Underutilization

- **Issue:**
  Inefficiently written GPU kernels can lead to poor utilization of the available computational resources.
- **Optimization Strategies:**
  - o **Memory Coalescing:** Ensure that threads access contiguous memory locations to optimize memory transactions.
  - o **Optimize Kernel Launch Parameters:** Experiment with different block and grid sizes to maximize GPU occupancy.
  - o **Use of Profiling Tools:** Tools such as NVIDIA Nsight Compute or AMD Radeon GPU Profiler can identify bottlenecks in kernel execution and suggest optimizations.

4. Synchronization Overhead

- **Issue:**
  Excessive synchronization between GPU threads can lead to idle cycles and decreased overall performance.

- **Optimization Strategies:**
  - **Minimize Barrier Synchronizations:** Only use synchronization primitives (e.g., __syncthreads() in CUDA) when absolutely necessary.
  - **Task Partitioning:** Design the computation to minimize dependencies between parallel tasks so that threads can work more independently.

5. Debugging and Code Complexity

- **Issue:**
  Debugging GPU code can be challenging due to its parallel and distributed nature.
- **Optimization Strategies:**
  - **Incremental Development:** Start with simple kernels and gradually add complexity, testing at each stage.
  - **Use of Debugging Tools:** Leverage GPU debuggers (e.g., CUDA-GDB, NVIDIA Nsight) and logging to identify issues.
  - **Modular Code Design:** Write modular, well-documented code to simplify maintenance and troubleshooting.

Summary Table: Common Challenges and Optimization Strategies

Challenge	Description	Optimization Strategies
Data Transfer Overhead	Slow transfers between host and GPU	Asynchronous transfers, pinned memory, GPU-based preprocessing
Memory Limitations	Limited GPU memory may restrict model size and resolution	Use lower precision, gradient checkpointing, parallelism
Kernel Inefficiencies	Poorly optimized kernels lead to underutilized cores	Memory coalescing, tuning block/grid sizes, profiling tools
Synchronization Overhead	Excessive synchronization reduces performance	Minimize barriers, improve task partitioning

Challenge	Description	Optimization Strategies
Debugging and Code Complexity	Parallel code is harder to debug and maintain	Incremental development, use of debugging tools, modular design

Real-World Example: Mixed-Precision Training

Mixed-precision training is an effective optimization strategy that leverages lower-precision arithmetic (e.g., FP16) alongside standard precision (FP32) to reduce memory usage and increase computational throughput.

Example: Implementing Mixed-Precision Training in PyTorch

```python
import torch
import torch.nn as nn
import torch.optim as optim
from torch.cuda.amp import GradScaler, autocast
from torchvision import datasets, transforms
from torchvision.models import resnet50

# Check for GPU availability
device = torch.device("cuda" if torch.cuda.is_available()
else "cpu")

# Load dataset (MNIST for simplicity)
transform = transforms.Compose([
    transforms.Resize((224, 224)),
    transforms.ToTensor(),
    transforms.Normalize(mean=[0.485], std=[0.229])
])
train_dataset = datasets.MNIST(root='./data', train=True,
download=True, transform=transform)
train_loader = torch.utils.data.DataLoader(train_dataset,
batch_size=64, shuffle=True)

# Define model and move to GPU
model = resnet50(pretrained=False, num_classes=10).to(device)

# Define loss function and optimizer
criterion = nn.CrossEntropyLoss()
optimizer = optim.Adam(model.parameters(), lr=0.001)
```

```
# Initialize GradScaler for mixed precision training
scaler = GradScaler()

# Training loop with mixed precision
model.train()
for epoch in range(5):  # 5 epochs for illustration
    for inputs, labels in train_loader:
        inputs, labels = inputs.to(device), labels.to(device)

        optimizer.zero_grad()

        # Use autocast to perform operations in mixed
precision
        with autocast():
            outputs = model(inputs)
            loss = criterion(outputs, labels)

        # Scale loss and backpropagate
        scaler.scale(loss).backward()
        scaler.step(optimizer)
        scaler.update()

    print(f"Epoch {epoch+1} completed.")
```

Explanation:

- **Mixed-Precision Setup:**
  The code uses `torch.cuda.amp.GradScaler` and
  `torch.cuda.amp.autocast` to enable mixed-precision training.
- **Benefits:**
  This approach reduces memory usage and increases throughput while
  maintaining model accuracy, illustrating one way to overcome
  memory and computational limitations.

6.6 Future Directions in AI and GPU Integration

As AI continues to evolve, the integration between GPU hardware and AI
algorithms is expected to deepen, driving new innovations and transforming
how models are built and deployed. In this section, we outline predictions
and emerging trends that represent the next frontier in AI hardware and
algorithm design.

Emerging Trends in AI Hardware

1. Specialized AI Accelerators

- **Dedicated AI Chips:**
  Beyond general-purpose GPUs, we can expect an increase in specialized AI accelerators designed explicitly for neural network workloads. Examples include Google's TPU (Tensor Processing Unit) and new generations of tensor cores.
- **Integration with GPUs:**
  Future systems may feature hybrid architectures that combine the versatility of GPUs with the efficiency of dedicated AI accelerators, providing the best of both worlds.

2. Neuromorphic Computing

- **Bio-Inspired Architectures:**
  Neuromorphic computing aims to mimic the structure and function of the human brain. These systems use spiking neural networks and can potentially operate at ultra-low power.
- **Potential Impact:**
  While still in early stages, neuromorphic chips could revolutionize tasks such as pattern recognition and sensory processing, complementing traditional GPU-accelerated AI.

3. Quantum-Enhanced AI

- **Quantum Computing Integration:**
  The integration of quantum computing elements with classical GPUs is a promising area of research. Quantum processors could handle specific optimization problems or search tasks that are computationally intensive.
- **Hybrid Models:**
  Future AI systems may employ hybrid models that leverage both classical GPU computing and quantum processing to achieve breakthroughs in areas like cryptography, material science, and complex decision-making.

4. Edge AI and Distributed Processing

- **Decentralized AI:**
  With the proliferation of IoT devices and 5G connectivity, AI is moving to the edge. GPUs designed for edge devices will need to balance power efficiency with performance.
- **Real-Time Inference:**
  Future edge AI solutions will rely on miniaturized, high-performance GPUs to enable real-time inference for applications such as autonomous vehicles, smart cameras, and augmented reality devices.

Algorithmic Innovations Driven by Future GPU Capabilities

1. Sparse and Quantized Neural Networks

- **Sparse Networks:**
  Future research is focusing on models that exploit sparsity to reduce the number of active parameters, making training and inference more efficient.
- **Quantization:**
  Lowering the precision of model weights and activations (e.g., using 8-bit or even lower precision) without sacrificing accuracy is an active area of research that can significantly reduce computational demands.

2. Adaptive and Self-Optimizing Models

- **Dynamic Architectures:**
  AI models of the future may incorporate mechanisms that allow them to adjust their architecture on-the-fly based on the complexity of the input data.
- **AutoML and Neural Architecture Search (NAS):**
  These techniques automate the design of neural networks, potentially leading to models that are more efficient and better tailored to the underlying hardware.

3. Integration of Multimodal Data

- **Unified Models:**
  The next generation of AI algorithms will increasingly integrate data from multiple modalities (e.g., text, images, audio, and sensor data) into a single coherent model.
- **GPU Role:**
  Advanced GPUs will be crucial in processing and fusing this diverse data efficiently, leading to richer, more context-aware AI systems.

Future Directions: Roadmap Summary

Trend/Innovation	Description	Potential Impact
Specialized AI Accelerators	Development of chips designed exclusively for AI workloads	Enhanced performance and efficiency for neural network training
Neuromorphic Computing	Bio-inspired architectures that mimic brain function	Ultra-low-power AI systems for real-time sensory processing
Quantum-Enhanced AI	Integration of quantum processors with classical GPUs	Breakthroughs in optimization and complex decision-making
Edge AI and Distributed Processing	High-performance, low-power GPUs for edge devices	Real-time inference and decentralized AI applications
Sparse and Quantized Networks	Models that leverage sparsity and lower-precision computations	Reduced computational cost and memory usage
Adaptive, Multimodal Models	Self-optimizing architectures that integrate diverse data types	Richer, more flexible AI systems that can learn from various inputs

Chapter Summary

In this final section of Chapter 6, we explored the challenges and future directions in GPU-driven AI. Section 6.5 discussed common pitfalls such as data transfer overhead, memory limitations, kernel inefficiencies, synchronization overhead, and debugging challenges. We provided practical strategies and a real-world example using mixed-precision training in PyTorch to illustrate how these issues can be mitigated.

Chapter 7: Performance Optimization and Benchmarking

Optimizing the performance of GPU-based applications is critical to harnessing the full potential of modern GPU architectures. Equally important is the ability to accurately benchmark and analyze performance to guide optimization efforts. In this chapter, we delve into the essential tools, methodologies, and best practices for profiling GPU performance and benchmarking against industry standards.

7.1 Profiling and Analyzing GPU Performance

Understanding the performance of your GPU-based applications is the first step in optimization. Profiling involves measuring various performance metrics to identify bottlenecks, inefficient resource utilization, and areas for improvement. This section introduces the key performance metrics, profiling tools, and diagnostic techniques used to analyze GPU performance.

Key Performance Metrics

When profiling GPU performance, several critical metrics should be monitored:

1. **Kernel Execution Time:**
   The time it takes for a GPU kernel (a function executed on the GPU) to complete. Shorter execution times generally indicate more efficient code.
2. **Memory Throughput:**
   The rate at which data is read from or written to the GPU's memory. High memory throughput is essential for data-intensive operations.
3. **Occupancy:**
   The ratio of active warps (groups of threads) to the maximum number of warps supported by a multiprocessor. Higher occupancy indicates better utilization of the GPU's computational resources.
4. **Latency:**
   The delay between initiating an operation and its completion. Lower latency improves responsiveness, particularly for real-time applications.

5. **Compute Utilization:**
   The percentage of the GPU's computational power that is being used. High compute utilization means the GPU is efficiently processing parallel tasks.

Diagnostic Tools for GPU Profiling

Several tools are available to help developers profile and analyze GPU performance. Here are some widely used tools:

- **NVIDIA Nsight Systems and Nsight Compute:**
  These tools provide detailed insights into kernel execution, memory usage, and overall GPU performance.
  - *Nsight Systems* offers a system-wide view, including CPU-GPU interactions, while
  - *Nsight Compute* focuses on kernel-level performance metrics.
- **AMD Radeon GPU Profiler:**
  This tool is designed for profiling AMD GPUs. It helps developers analyze shader performance, memory access patterns, and pipeline utilization.
- **Intel Graphics Performance Analyzers (GPA):**
  A suite of tools for profiling and debugging Intel GPUs, offering real-time performance insights and optimization recommendations.
- **Open-source Tools:**
  Tools like **nvprof** (for NVIDIA GPUs) and **ROCprof** (for AMD GPUs) are also available and provide command-line interfaces for performance analysis.

Practical Example: Using NVIDIA Nsight Compute

Below is a simplified example demonstrating how to use NVIDIA Nsight Compute for profiling a CUDA kernel.

Step 1: Compile the CUDA Program

Assume you have a CUDA program named `matrixMul.cu`. Compile it with debugging symbols enabled:

```bash
nvcc -G -lineinfo -o matrixMul matrixMul.cu
```

- **Explanation:**
  The `-G` flag enables debugging information, and `-lineinfo` provides source code line mapping to the generated code, which is useful during profiling.

Step 2: Run Nsight Compute

Launch Nsight Compute from the command line to profile the `matrixMul` executable:

```bash
ncu --set full --target-processes all ./matrixMul
```

- **Explanation:**
  The `--set full` flag specifies a detailed profiling session, and `--target-processes all` ensures that all GPU processes are monitored.

Step 3: Analyze the Report

Nsight Compute generates a report with detailed metrics such as kernel execution time, occupancy, memory throughput, and more. Review the report to identify potential bottlenecks.

Summary Table: Common GPU Performance Metrics

Metric	Description	Why It Matters
Kernel Execution Time	Time taken for a GPU kernel to complete	Indicates efficiency of GPU code; shorter is better
Memory Throughput	Data transfer rate between GPU memory and cores	High throughput is essential for data-intensive tasks
Occupancy	Ratio of active warps to maximum supported warps	Higher occupancy generally means better resource utilization
Latency	Delay between initiating and completing an operation	Lower latency improves responsiveness for real-time tasks

Metric	Description	Why It Matters
Compute Utilization	Percentage of the GPU's computational capacity used	Higher utilization indicates efficient use of hardware

7.2 Benchmarking Methodologies and Industry Standards

Benchmarking is the process of evaluating the performance of a GPU or GPU-accelerated application against established standards or other systems. This section outlines best practices for benchmarking, key methodologies, and industry standards that ensure meaningful and comparable results.

Best Practices for Benchmarking GPUs

1. **Use Standardized Workloads:**
   Benchmarking should be performed using standardized, well-understood workloads. These may include synthetic benchmarks (e.g., FLOPS tests, memory throughput tests) and real-world applications (e.g., gaming or deep learning training).
2. **Control Environmental Variables:**
   Ensure that benchmarks are conducted under consistent conditions. This includes controlling factors such as ambient temperature, background processes, and system configurations.
3. **Multiple Runs and Statistical Analysis:**
   Run benchmarks multiple times and analyze the average performance and variance. This helps account for variability and ensures that results are statistically significant.
4. **Report Comprehensive Metrics:**
   Include both computational and memory performance metrics, as well as power consumption and thermal data if applicable. Comprehensive reporting provides a holistic view of GPU performance.
5. **Utilize Benchmark Suites:**
   Use established benchmark suites such as SPECviewperf, 3DMark, or MLPerf (for machine learning) to ensure that results are comparable across different systems and vendors.

Benchmarking Methodologies

Synthetic Benchmarks

- **Purpose:**
  Synthetic benchmarks are designed to isolate specific aspects of GPU performance, such as floating-point computation, memory bandwidth, or shader efficiency.
- **Examples:**
  - **FLOPS Benchmark:** Measures the floating-point operations per second.
  - **Memory Bandwidth Tests:** Evaluate the speed of data transfer between GPU memory and cores.
- **Advantages:**
  Synthetic benchmarks provide clear, quantifiable metrics that can be easily compared across systems.

Real-World Application Benchmarks

- **Purpose:**
  These benchmarks evaluate performance using actual applications or workloads, such as gaming, deep learning training, or video rendering.
- **Examples:**
  - **Gaming Benchmarks:** Measure frame rates, latency, and visual quality in real-time gaming scenarios.
  - **MLPerf:** A suite of benchmarks for evaluating the performance of machine learning systems.
- **Advantages:**
  Real-world benchmarks provide insights into how well a GPU performs in practical, everyday use cases.

Industry Standards and Benchmark Suites

Several industry-standard benchmark suites have been developed to provide consistent and comparable performance metrics for GPUs:

- **SPECviewperf:**
  A benchmark suite focused on 3D graphics performance, widely used in the professional graphics industry.

- **3DMark:**
  A popular benchmark for evaluating gaming performance, providing scores based on synthetic tests that simulate gaming workloads.
- **MLPerf:**
  A benchmark suite specifically designed for machine learning, covering a wide range of tasks including image classification, object detection, and language processing.
- **An Example Workflow for MLPerf Benchmarking:**
  1. **Setup:**
     Install the MLPerf benchmark suite and configure it for your target hardware and workload (e.g., training a ResNet model).
  2. **Run Benchmarks:**
     Execute the benchmark tests while ensuring that system settings (e.g., power modes, thermal conditions) are controlled.
  3. **Collect Data:**
     Gather metrics such as training time, inference latency, and accuracy.
  4. **Analyze and Compare:**
     Compare your results against published MLPerf scores to gauge the relative performance of your system.

Summary Table: Benchmarking Methodologies and Tools

Methodology	Description	Examples/Tools
Synthetic Benchmarks	Isolate and measure specific GPU capabilities (e.g., FLOPS, memory bandwidth)	FLOPS tests, memory bandwidth benchmarks
Real-World Application Benchmarks	Evaluate GPU performance using actual applications or workloads	Gaming benchmarks (3DMark), MLPerf for machine learning
Industry Standards	Established benchmarks ensuring consistent and comparable results	SPECviewperf, 3DMark, MLPerf
Best Practices	Guidelines for controlled, repeatable, and comprehensive benchmarking	Multiple runs, environmental control, statistical analysis

Practical Example: Benchmarking a GPU-Accelerated Application

Consider a deep learning training script for a CNN model. To benchmark this application:

1. **Baseline Measurement:**
   Run the training script on a reference GPU and record key metrics (e.g., training time per epoch, GPU utilization, memory throughput).
2. **Optimization Iterations:**
   Apply a series of optimizations (e.g., mixed-precision training, kernel tuning) and re-run the benchmarks. Compare the results to the baseline.
3. **Profiling Integration:**
   Use profiling tools (e.g., NVIDIA Nsight Compute) to correlate improvements with specific optimizations.
4. **Documentation:**
   Document the setup, environmental conditions, and hardware configurations to ensure that the benchmark results are reproducible and comparable.

7.3 Memory, Compute, and Data Transfer Optimizations

Optimizing performance in GPU-based applications often requires addressing bottlenecks in memory, computation, and data transfers. In this section, we detail a range of techniques that can be applied to reduce these bottlenecks and maximize throughput.

Memory Optimizations

1. Memory Coalescing

Concept:
Memory coalescing occurs when threads in a warp access contiguous memory locations, enabling the GPU to combine these individual accesses into a single, efficient transaction.

Implementation Tips:

- **Data Layout:** Organize data in memory so that consecutive threads access consecutive memory addresses.
- **Aligned Memory Access:** Ensure that arrays and data structures are properly aligned with the GPU's memory architecture.

Example:
When processing an array in CUDA, ensure that thread `i` accesses element `A[i]`. This promotes coalescing, which minimizes the number of memory transactions.

Shared Memory Utilization

Concept:
Shared memory is an on-chip memory that is much faster than global memory. Using shared memory effectively can greatly reduce latency for frequently accessed data.

Strategies:

- **Tiling:** Divide data into small tiles that fit into shared memory. For example, in matrix multiplication, load blocks of matrices into shared memory before performing computations.
- **Avoiding Bank Conflicts:** Organize data access patterns to minimize simultaneous access to the same memory bank.

Example: Tiled Matrix Multiplication

```cpp
__global__ void tiledMatrixMul(const float *A, const float *B, float *C, int N) {
    // Define shared memory arrays for tiles from A and B
    __shared__ float tileA[16][16];
    __shared__ float tileB[16][16];

    int row = blockIdx.y * blockDim.y + threadIdx.y;
    int col = blockIdx.x * blockDim.x + threadIdx.x;
    float value = 0.0f;
```

```
    // Loop over tiles
    for (int t = 0; t < (N + 15) / 16; t++) {
        // Load data into shared memory
        if (row < N && t * 16 + threadIdx.x < N)
            tileA[threadIdx.y][threadIdx.x] = A[row * N + t *
16 + threadIdx.x];
        else
            tileA[threadIdx.y][threadIdx.x] = 0.0f;

        if (col < N && t * 16 + threadIdx.y < N)
            tileB[threadIdx.y][threadIdx.x] = B[(t * 16 +
threadIdx.y) * N + col];
        else
            tileB[threadIdx.y][threadIdx.x] = 0.0f;

        __syncthreads();

        // Perform multiplication for the tile
        for (int i = 0; i < 16; i++) {
            value += tileA[threadIdx.y][i] *
tileB[i][threadIdx.x];
        }
        __syncthreads();
    }
    if (row < N && col < N)
        C[row * N + col] = value;
}
```

Explanation:

- **Tiling:** The kernel divides the matrices into 16×16 tiles that are loaded into shared memory.
- **Synchronization:** The __syncthreads() call ensures that all threads complete loading data before computation begins.
- **Result:** This method minimizes global memory accesses and maximizes reuse of data within fast shared memory.

Compute Optimizations

1. Kernel Fusion

Concept:
Kernel fusion involves combining multiple small kernels into a single kernel.

This reduces the overhead of launching multiple kernels and improves data locality.

Benefits:

- **Reduced Overhead:** Fewer kernel launches mean less time spent in scheduling and context switching.
- **Improved Data Reuse:** Data loaded into fast memory can be reused across multiple operations within the same kernel.

2. Loop Unrolling and Instruction-Level Parallelism

Concept:
Loop unrolling reduces the overhead of loop control and increases instruction-level parallelism by duplicating the loop body multiple times.

Implementation Tips:

- **Manual Unrolling:** Unroll small loops manually to improve performance, especially in compute-intensive kernels.
- **Compiler Directives:** Use compiler directives or pragmas to guide the compiler to unroll loops where beneficial.

Data Transfer Optimizations

1. Asynchronous Data Transfers

Concept:
Asynchronous data transfers allow data to be moved between host and device concurrently with kernel execution, thereby overlapping computation and communication.

Implementation Tips:

- **CUDA Streams:** Use CUDA streams to perform non-blocking memory copies.
- **Double Buffering:** Implement double buffering to ensure that one buffer is used for computation while the other is being filled with new data.

Example: Asynchronous Memory Copy in CUDA

cpp

```cpp
cudaStream_t stream;
cudaStreamCreate(&stream);
cudaMemcpyAsync(d_input, h_input, size,
cudaMemcpyHostToDevice, stream);
// Launch kernel on the same stream
myKernel<<<gridDim, blockDim, 0, stream>>>(d_input,
d_output);
// Copy result back asynchronously
cudaMemcpyAsync(h_output, d_output, size,
cudaMemcpyDeviceToHost, stream);
cudaStreamSynchronize(stream);
cudaStreamDestroy(stream);
```

Explanation:

- **Streams:** The code creates a CUDA stream for asynchronous operations.
- **Overlap:** Data transfer and kernel execution occur concurrently, reducing overall latency.

2. Reducing Data Transfer Frequency

Strategies:

- **On-GPU Preprocessing:** Process and augment data directly on the GPU to reduce the need for frequent data transfers.
- **Batching:** Transfer larger batches of data at once rather than many small transfers, which minimizes overhead.

7.4 Real-World Performance Case Studies

Real-world case studies provide insight into how optimization strategies can significantly improve application performance. Below are a few examples that illustrate the impact of various optimizations.

Case Study 1: Deep Learning Training Acceleration

Scenario:
Training a deep neural network for image classification on the ImageNet dataset.

Optimizations Applied:

- **Mixed-Precision Training:** Reduced memory usage and increased throughput.
- **Data Parallelism:** Distributed mini-batches across multiple GPUs.
- **Efficient Data Loading:** Implemented asynchronous data loading and preprocessing on the GPU.

Results:

- **Training Time:** Reduced from 24 hours to 12 hours.
- **GPU Utilization:** Increased from 65% to 90%.
- **Memory Bandwidth:** Improved by 25% through memory coalescing and shared memory usage.

Case Study 2: Real-Time Ray Tracing in Gaming

Scenario:
A next-generation gaming engine implementing real-time ray tracing for realistic lighting.

Optimizations Applied:

- **Ray Tracing Core Utilization:** Leveraged specialized hardware units for ray tracing calculations.
- **Kernel Fusion:** Combined shading and ray intersection calculations into a single kernel.
- **Asynchronous Data Transfers:** Used asynchronous transfers to feed scene data to the GPU.

Results:

- **Frame Rate:** Increased from 30 FPS to 60 FPS.
- **Latency:** Reduced by 20%, leading to smoother gameplay.

- **Power Efficiency:** Improved by 15% due to optimized kernel usage and reduced memory transfers.

Case Study 3: Scientific Simulation Application

Scenario:
A fluid dynamics simulation requiring large-scale parallel computation.

Optimizations Applied:

- **Tiled Computation:** Implemented tiling in shared memory to optimize data reuse.
- **Loop Unrolling:** Unrolled critical loops to maximize instruction-level parallelism.
- **Pipelined Data Transfer:** Overlapped data transfer with computation using double buffering.

Results:

- **Simulation Speed:** Increased by 40%.
- **Compute Utilization:** Enhanced to near-maximum GPU occupancy.
- **Memory Throughput:** Improved by 30%, reducing overall simulation time.

Summary Table: Real-World Performance Improvements

Application	Optimizations Applied	Performance Gains
Deep Learning Training	Mixed-precision, data parallelism, asynchronous data loading	50% reduction in training time, increased utilization
Real-Time Ray Tracing	Ray tracing cores, kernel fusion, asynchronous data transfers	Doubling of frame rate, reduced latency
Scientific Simulation	Tiling, loop unrolling, pipelined data transfer	40% faster simulation speed, improved throughput

7.5 Balancing Performance, Efficiency, and Cost

Optimizing a system is not solely about achieving the highest performance; it also involves balancing performance with efficiency and cost. Here, we discuss strategies for achieving an optimal design that meets application requirements while considering power, thermal, and economic constraints.

Key Considerations

1. **Performance vs. Power Consumption:**
   - **Trade-Off:** Higher performance often requires higher power consumption, which can lead to increased heat generation and operating costs.
   - **Strategies:**
     - **Dynamic Voltage and Frequency Scaling (DVFS):** Adjusts GPU performance based on workload demand.
     - **Power Gating:** Shuts down unused cores to save power during low-demand periods.
2. **Cost vs. Performance:**
   - **Trade-Off:** Cutting-edge GPUs deliver high performance but come at a premium cost.
   - **Strategies:**
     - **Scalability:** Use multi-GPU configurations or distributed systems to achieve high performance without relying on a single high-end GPU.
     - **Workload Matching:** Choose the GPU configuration that best matches the workload requirements; not every application needs the highest-end hardware.
3. **Thermal Management and Efficiency:**
   - **Trade-Off:** Aggressive performance tuning can lead to thermal challenges that may affect system reliability.
   - **Strategies:**
     - **Advanced Cooling Solutions:** Implement liquid cooling or improved airflow designs.
     - **Thermal Throttling:** Use built-in throttling mechanisms to prevent overheating while maintaining acceptable performance levels.

Balancing Strategies

- **Holistic System Design:**
  Consider the entire system—including CPU, memory, storage, and cooling—when optimizing for performance. An imbalanced system may suffer from bottlenecks even if the GPU is highly optimized.
- **Benchmarking and Simulation:**
  Use benchmarking tools to simulate real-world workloads and determine the optimal balance between performance, power consumption, and cost. Iterative testing helps identify the "sweet spot" for system configurations.
- **Modular Scalability:**
  Design systems that can be scaled modularly. For instance, start with a baseline configuration and add additional GPUs or processing nodes as needed, ensuring that the system remains cost-effective as performance demands grow.

Summary Table: Balancing Performance, Efficiency, and Cost

Aspect	Consideration	Optimization Strategy
Performance vs. Power	Higher performance can lead to increased power usage and heat	DVFS, power gating, efficient kernel design
Cost vs. Performance	High-end GPUs offer superior performance at higher cost	Scalable multi-GPU configurations, workload-specific hardware selection
Thermal Management	High performance may cause thermal issues affecting reliability	Advanced cooling solutions, thermal throttling, balanced system design

Chapter Summary

In Chapter 7, we explored a comprehensive range of techniques for optimizing GPU performance and accurately benchmarking systems to achieve the best balance of memory, compute, and data transfer efficiencies.

Chapter 8: Programming and Developing for Advanced GPU Architectures

In this chapter, we delve into the software side of GPU technology by exploring programming models and advanced programming techniques that enable developers to harness the full power of modern GPUs. We begin with an in-depth overview of the primary GPU programming APIs, comparing their features, use cases, and ecosystem support. Then, we focus on advanced CUDA programming techniques, offering strategies and examples to optimize code for maximum performance and efficiency.

8.1 In-Depth Overview of GPU Programming Models

GPU programming models provide the interfaces and tools needed to develop applications that can exploit the massive parallelism offered by modern GPUs. The most widely used models include CUDA, OpenCL, Vulkan, and others. Understanding their differences, strengths, and appropriate use cases is crucial for selecting the right tool for your project.

Key Programming Models

API/Model	Developed By	Primary Language	Key Features	Typical Use Cases
CUDA	NVIDIA	C/C++ (with extensions)	- Dedicated to NVIDIA GPUs - Extensive libraries (cuDNN, cuBLAS, etc.) - Rich developer tools and debugging support (Nsight)	High-performance computing, deep learning, scientific simulations

API/Model	Developed By	Primary Language	Key Features	Typical Use Cases
OpenCL	Khronos Group	C-based language	- Platform-agnostic: supports CPUs, GPUs, FPGAs, and more - Enables heterogeneous computing - Portable across multiple vendors	Cross-platform parallel programming, heterogeneous computing
Vulkan	Khronos Group	C/C++ (with SPIR-V shaders)	- Low-level API for graphics and compute - Explicit control over GPU resources - High efficiency with reduced driver overhead	Real-time graphics, gaming, compute-intensive graphics applications
DirectCompute	Microsoft	HLSL (High-Level Shading Language)	- Part of the DirectX family - Provides compute shader capabilities - Integrated with Windows platforms	Windows-specific compute applications, gaming, multimedia
SYCL	Khronos Group (and community initiatives)	C++	- Single-source programming model for heterogeneous computing - Combines host and device code in one	Academic research, rapid prototyping, cross-platform development

API/Model	Developed By	Primary Language	Key Features	Typical Use Cases
			C++ file - Builds on OpenCL for portability	

Comparison and Considerations

CUDA

- **Strengths:**
  - Optimized specifically for NVIDIA hardware.
  - Extensive ecosystem, with libraries such as cuDNN, TensorRT, and cuBLAS accelerating development in deep learning and HPC.
  - Mature development tools (Nsight Systems, Nsight Compute) that provide detailed performance analysis.
- **Limitations:**
  - Vendor lock-in: Only works on NVIDIA GPUs.
  - Proprietary platform with licensing considerations.

OpenCL

- **Strengths:**
  - Cross-platform support across GPUs, CPUs, and other accelerators.
  - Enables heterogeneous computing, which is ideal for environments with mixed hardware.
- **Limitations:**
  - Can be more challenging to optimize for specific hardware compared to vendor-specific APIs.
  - Fragmented ecosystem; performance may vary across devices.

Vulkan

- **Strengths:**
  - Provides low-level control over GPU resources, which can yield high performance if used correctly.
  - Unified API for both graphics and compute operations.

- **Limitations:**
  - Higher complexity; requires more boilerplate code to manage resources.
  - Learning curve is steeper compared to higher-level APIs like CUDA.

DirectCompute

- **Strengths:**
  - Seamlessly integrates with other DirectX APIs.
  - Suitable for Windows-centric applications.
- **Limitations:**
  - Limited to the Windows platform.
  - Not as widely adopted for general-purpose computing compared to CUDA or OpenCL.

SYCL

- **Strengths:**
  - Single-source approach makes it easier to manage code for both host and device.
  - Builds on OpenCL for portability while offering modern C++ features.
- **Limitations:**
  - Newer and less mature compared to CUDA.
  - Ecosystem and tool support are still developing.

Code Example: Simple Vector Addition in CUDA and OpenCL

CUDA Example

cpp

```
// CUDA Kernel for vector addition
__global__ void vectorAdd(const float *A, const float *B,
float *C, int N) {
    int idx = blockIdx.x * blockDim.x + threadIdx.x;
    if (idx < N) {
        C[idx] = A[idx] + B[idx];
    }
}

#include <iostream>
#include <cuda_runtime.h>
```

```cpp
int main() {
    int N = 1024;
    size_t size = N * sizeof(float);
    float *h_A = (float *)malloc(size);
    float *h_B = (float *)malloc(size);
    float *h_C = (float *)malloc(size);

    // Initialize host arrays
    for (int i = 0; i < N; i++) {
        h_A[i] = static_cast<float>(i);
        h_B[i] = static_cast<float>(N - i);
    }

    float *d_A, *d_B, *d_C;
    cudaMalloc(&d_A, size);
    cudaMalloc(&d_B, size);
    cudaMalloc(&d_C, size);

    cudaMemcpy(d_A, h_A, size, cudaMemcpyHostToDevice);
    cudaMemcpy(d_B, h_B, size, cudaMemcpyHostToDevice);

    int threadsPerBlock = 256;
    int blocksPerGrid = (N + threadsPerBlock - 1) /
threadsPerBlock;
    vectorAdd<<<blocksPerGrid, threadsPerBlock>>>(d_A, d_B,
d_C, N);

    cudaMemcpy(h_C, d_C, size, cudaMemcpyDeviceToHost);

    // Verify results (omitted for brevity)
    std::cout << "Vector addition completed." << std::endl;

    cudaFree(d_A);
    cudaFree(d_B);
    cudaFree(d_C);
    free(h_A);
    free(h_B);
    free(h_C);
    return 0;
}
```

OpenCL Example

```c
c

// OpenCL Kernel for vector addition
const char *kernelSource =
"__kernel void vectorAdd(__global const float *A, __global
const float *B, __global float *C, int N) {"
```

```c
"    int idx = get_global_id(0);"
"    if (idx < N) {"
"        C[idx] = A[idx] + B[idx];"
"    }"
"}";

#include <stdio.h>
#include <stdlib.h>
#include <CL/cl.h>

int main() {
    int N = 1024;
    size_t size = N * sizeof(float);
    float *h_A = (float *)malloc(size);
    float *h_B = (float *)malloc(size);
    float *h_C = (float *)malloc(size);

    // Initialize host arrays
    for (int i = 0; i < N; i++) {
        h_A[i] = (float)i;
        h_B[i] = (float)(N - i);
    }

    // OpenCL setup: Get platform/device, create context,
command queue, program, kernel (omitted for brevity)
    // Assume cl_context, cl_command_queue, cl_program, and
cl_kernel are properly created.

    // Create buffers, set kernel arguments, and enqueue
kernel (pseudocode)
    // clSetKernelArg(kernel, 0, sizeof(cl_mem), (void
*)&d_A);
    // clSetKernelArg(kernel, 1, sizeof(cl_mem), (void
*)&d_B);
    // clSetKernelArg(kernel, 2, sizeof(cl_mem), (void
*)&d_C);
    // clSetKernelArg(kernel, 3, sizeof(int), &N);
    // size_t globalSize = N;
    // clEnqueueNDRangeKernel(command_queue, kernel, 1, NULL,
&globalSize, NULL, 0, NULL, NULL);

    // Read results back from device
    // clEnqueueReadBuffer(command_queue, d_C, CL_TRUE, 0,
size, h_C, 0, NULL, NULL);

    printf("Vector addition completed using OpenCL.\n");

    // Cleanup OpenCL objects and free memory (omitted for
brevity)
    free(h_A);
    free(h_B);
```

```
    free(h_C);
    return 0;
}
```

Explanation:

- **CUDA Example:**
  The CUDA code defines a simple kernel for vector addition, allocates memory on the device, transfers data, executes the kernel, and retrieves the results.
- **OpenCL Example:**
  The OpenCL code shows the kernel source as a string and outlines the typical steps: setting up the platform, creating the context, compiling the kernel, setting kernel arguments, and executing the kernel. Detailed setup steps are omitted for brevity but follow standard OpenCL API usage.

8.2 Advanced CUDA Programming Techniques

After selecting a programming model, the next step is to optimize your code for maximum performance and efficiency. CUDA, as the leading API for NVIDIA GPUs, offers a range of advanced techniques to extract peak performance from the hardware.

1. Optimizing Memory Access

Memory Coalescing

- **Concept:**
  Ensure that threads within a warp access contiguous memory locations.
- **Implementation Tip:**
  Organize data structures so that thread i accesses the ith element of an array. This allows multiple memory accesses to be merged into a single transaction.

Shared Memory Usage

- **Concept:**
  Use shared memory to store frequently accessed data that is common among threads.
- **Example:**
  In tiled matrix multiplication (shown earlier), loading tiles of data into shared memory minimizes global memory accesses and improves performance.

Avoiding Bank Conflicts

- **Concept:**
  Arrange data in shared memory to prevent multiple threads from accessing the same memory bank simultaneously.
- **Implementation Tip:**
  Use padding in shared memory arrays if necessary to avoid conflicts.

2. Kernel Optimization Techniques

Kernel Fusion

- **Concept:**
  Merge multiple kernels into one to reduce kernel launch overhead and improve data locality.
- **Benefits:**
  Fewer kernel launches reduce latency, and data can be reused without transferring between kernels.

Loop Unrolling

- **Concept:**
  Manually or automatically unroll loops to reduce loop control overhead and increase instruction-level parallelism.
- **Example:**
  For a small fixed-size loop inside a kernel, unroll it to eliminate branch instructions.

Using Intrinsics

- **Concept:**
  Use low-level CUDA intrinsics for certain operations to achieve faster performance.

- **Example:**
  Functions like `__fmaf_rn(a, b, c)` compute fused multiply-add operations, which can be more efficient than separate multiplication and addition.

3. Asynchronous Execution and Streams

Overlapping Computation and Data Transfer

- **Concept:**
  Use CUDA streams to overlap data transfers between host and device with kernel execution.
- **Example:**
  The asynchronous memory copy example in Section 7.3 demonstrates how to create a CUDA stream and use `cudaMemcpyAsync` to perform data transfers concurrently with kernel execution.

4. Profiling and Iterative Optimization

Use of Profiling Tools

- **Tools:**
  NVIDIA Nsight Compute, Nsight Systems, and nvprof can provide detailed insights into kernel performance.
- **Method:**
  Profile your code to identify hotspots and then apply targeted optimizations. For instance, if occupancy is low, consider adjusting your kernel's thread block size.

Iterative Tuning

- **Concept:**
  Optimization is often an iterative process. Make a change, profile the performance, and repeat.
- **Example Workflow:**
  1. Profile the kernel to measure execution time and occupancy.
  2. Adjust block and grid dimensions.
  3. Apply memory optimizations (e.g., shared memory tiling).
  4. Re-profile and compare results.

Code Example: Optimized CUDA Kernel Using Shared Memory and Loop Unrolling

Below is an example of an optimized CUDA kernel for vector addition that uses loop unrolling to reduce loop overhead. Although vector addition is simple, this example illustrates the application of advanced techniques.

cpp

```cpp
// Optimized CUDA Kernel for Vector Addition with Loop
Unrolling
__global__ void vectorAddOptimized(const float *A, const
float *B, float *C, int N) {
    int idx = blockIdx.x * blockDim.x + threadIdx.x;
    // Process multiple elements per thread using loop
unrolling
    int stride = blockDim.x * gridDim.x;
    for (int i = idx; i < N; i += stride * 4) {
        // Unroll loop by a factor of 4, ensuring we don't
exceed N
        if (i < N)
            C[i] = A[i] + B[i];
        if (i + stride < N)
            C[i + stride] = A[i + stride] + B[i + stride];
        if (i + 2 * stride < N)
            C[i + 2 * stride] = A[i + 2 * stride] + B[i + 2 *
stride];
        if (i + 3 * stride < N)
            C[i + 3 * stride] = A[i + 3 * stride] + B[i + 3 *
stride];
    }
}

#include <iostream>
#include <cuda_runtime.h>

int main() {
    int N = 1 << 20; // 1M elements
    size_t size = N * sizeof(float);
    float *h_A = (float *)malloc(size);
    float *h_B = (float *)malloc(size);
    float *h_C = (float *)malloc(size);

    // Initialize host arrays
    for (int i = 0; i < N; i++) {
        h_A[i] = static_cast<float>(i);
        h_B[i] = static_cast<float>(2 * i);
    }
```

```
    float *d_A, *d_B, *d_C;
    cudaMalloc(&d_A, size);
    cudaMalloc(&d_B, size);
    cudaMalloc(&d_C, size);

    cudaMemcpy(d_A, h_A, size, cudaMemcpyHostToDevice);
    cudaMemcpy(d_B, h_B, size, cudaMemcpyHostToDevice);

    int threadsPerBlock = 256;
    int blocksPerGrid = (N + threadsPerBlock - 1) /
threadsPerBlock;
    vectorAddOptimized<<<blocksPerGrid,
threadsPerBlock>>>(d_A, d_B, d_C, N);

    cudaMemcpy(h_C, d_C, size, cudaMemcpyDeviceToHost);

    // Verify results (omitted for brevity)
    std::cout << "Optimized vector addition completed." <<
std::endl;

    cudaFree(d_A);
    cudaFree(d_B);
    cudaFree(d_C);
    free(h_A);
    free(h_B);
    free(h_C);
    return 0;
}
```

Explanation:

- **Loop Unrolling:**
  The kernel processes four elements per thread per iteration, reducing
  the loop overhead.
- **Stride Calculation:**
  Threads work in a strided manner to cover all elements in the array.
- **Benefits:**
  This approach can improve performance by reducing the number of
  iterations and increasing instruction-level parallelism.

Summary Table: Advanced CUDA Optimization Techniques

Technique	Description	Benefits
Memory Coalescing	Ensuring contiguous memory accesses by threads	Reduced memory transactions, increased throughput

Technique	Description	Benefits
Shared Memory Utilization	Using on-chip memory to store frequently accessed data	Lower latency, improved data reuse
Kernel Fusion	Merging multiple kernels into one	Reduced launch overhead, improved data locality
Loop Unrolling	Manually or automatically unrolling loops	Reduced loop overhead, increased parallelism
Asynchronous Execution	Overlapping data transfers with computation using CUDA streams	Reduced overall latency, better GPU utilization
Profiling and Iterative Tuning	Using tools like Nsight Compute to guide optimizations	Targeted improvements based on measured performance

8.3 Emerging Programming Paradigms and Languages

The landscape of GPU programming is continuously evolving as new paradigms and languages emerge to simplify development, enhance performance, and expand cross-platform compatibility. In this section, we explore some of the latest trends and tools that are reshaping the way developers interact with GPU hardware.

New Paradigms in GPU Programming

1. Single-Source Programming Models

Concept:
Single-source programming allows developers to write host (CPU) and device (GPU) code in the same source file, simplifying development and maintenance.

Example: SYCL

- **Overview:**
  SYCL is a high-level, single-source programming model built on top

of OpenCL. It leverages modern C++ features, enabling developers to write cleaner and more maintainable code that is portable across different hardware platforms.

- **Key Benefits:**
    - o **Code Simplicity:** Integrates host and device code seamlessly.
    - o **Portability:** Supports a range of devices including GPUs, CPUs, and FPGAs.
    - o **Modern C++ Support:** Allows the use of modern language features such as lambdas and templates.

Code Example: Simple Vector Addition in SYCL

```cpp
#include <CL/sycl.hpp>
#include <iostream>
using namespace sycl;

int main() {
    const size_t N = 1024;
    float *A = new float[N];
    float *B = new float[N];
    float *C = new float[N];

    // Initialize arrays
    for (size_t i = 0; i < N; ++i) {
        A[i] = static_cast<float>(i);
        B[i] = static_cast<float>(N - i);
    }

    {
        // Create a SYCL queue to submit work to the default
device (GPU if available)
        queue q;
        buffer<float, 1> bufA(A, range<1>(N));
        buffer<float, 1> bufB(B, range<1>(N));
        buffer<float, 1> bufC(C, range<1>(N));

        q.submit([&](handler &h) {
            auto accA =
bufA.get_access<access::mode::read>(h);
            auto accB =
bufB.get_access<access::mode::read>(h);
            auto accC =
bufC.get_access<access::mode::write>(h);
            h.parallel_for(range<1>(N), [=](id<1> i) {
                accC[i] = accA[i] + accB[i];
            });
```

```
        });
        q.wait(); // Ensure all operations complete before
exiting the scope
    }

    // Output result for verification
    std::cout << "C[0] = " << C[0] << "\nC[N-1] = " << C[N-1]
<< std::endl;

    delete[] A;
    delete[] B;
    delete[] C;
    return 0;
}
```

Explanation:

- The code uses SYCL to perform vector addition, combining host and device code in one file.
- The `queue` object abstracts device selection, and buffers manage memory transfers automatically.
- The `parallel_for` function distributes the vector addition across available GPU threads.

2. Low-Level, Cross-Platform APIs

Vulkan Compute:

- **Overview:**
  Initially designed for high-performance graphics, Vulkan has expanded to include compute capabilities.
- **Key Benefits:**
  - **Low Overhead:** Provides explicit control over GPU resources, reducing driver overhead.
  - **Cross-Platform:** Supported on various operating systems, making it a strong candidate for applications requiring both graphics and compute.
- **Challenges:**
  - **Complexity:** Requires more boilerplate code and a deeper understanding of GPU hardware.

Emerging Languages:

- **OpenACC:**
  A directive-based approach that allows developers to annotate existing C/C++ or Fortran code with pragmas to offload compute-intensive sections to the GPU.
- **CUDA C++ Updates:**
  Continued evolution of CUDA includes enhanced support for C++ features, libraries, and improved interoperability with other programming models, ensuring that developers can leverage modern language constructs.

3. Domain-Specific Languages (DSLs)

Concept:
DSLs tailored for GPU computing simplify the process of expressing parallelism for specific domains, such as linear algebra or image processing.

- **Examples:**
  - **Halide:**
    A language designed for image processing that allows developers to separate algorithm specification from scheduling, enabling automatic optimization for GPU architectures.
  - **TVM:**
    An open deep learning compiler stack that optimizes and generates code for various hardware backends, including GPUs.

Summary Table: Emerging Programming Paradigms and Languages

Paradigm/Language	Key Features	Primary Use Cases
SYCL	Single-source, modern C++ support, portable across devices	Heterogeneous computing, cross-platform development
Vulkan Compute	Low-level API with explicit resource control, cross-platform	High-performance graphics and compute applications
OpenACC	Directive-based, minimal code changes, accelerates existing code	Scientific computing, legacy code modernization

Paradigm/Language	Key Features	Primary Use Cases
Domain-Specific Languages (Halide, TVM)	Focused on specific domains with automatic optimizations	Image processing, deep learning model deployment

8.4 Debugging and Tuning GPU Applications

Even with powerful tools and advanced techniques, debugging and tuning GPU applications can be challenging due to their inherent parallelism and complexity. This section outlines best practices, techniques, and tools to help identify and solve performance issues in GPU applications.

Best Practices for Debugging GPU Applications

1. Incremental Development and Testing

Strategy:
Develop and test your GPU kernels incrementally:

- **Start Simple:** Begin with a simple version of your kernel and verify its correctness.
- **Add Complexity Gradually:** Introduce optimizations and additional features step-by-step, testing each change for correctness and performance impact.

2. Use of Debugging Tools

NVIDIA Nsight and CUDA-GDB:

- **Nsight Compute:**
  Provides detailed profiling and analysis of individual kernels, including memory usage, occupancy, and execution time.
- **CUDA-GDB:**
  A debugger tailored for CUDA applications, allowing you to step through GPU code and inspect variables.

- **Other Tools:**
  Tools such as AMD Radeon GPU Profiler and Intel Graphics Performance Analyzers are available for their respective platforms.

3. Logging and Error Checking

Techniques:

- **Error Checking:**
  Always check the return values of CUDA API calls (e.g., `cudaMalloc`, `cudaMemcpy`). Use helper macros to catch errors early.
- **Logging:**
  Insert logging statements in both host and device code (using techniques such as writing to a buffer that is later copied back to the host) to diagnose issues in kernel execution.

4. Simulated Environments and Emulators

Usage:

- **GPU Emulators:**
  While not a replacement for real hardware, GPU emulators can help in debugging by providing a controlled environment where race conditions and memory issues can be identified.
- **Unit Testing Frameworks:**
  Incorporate unit tests for individual kernels to ensure they perform as expected before integrating them into larger applications.

Tuning GPU Applications for Performance

1. Profiling and Analysis

Tools:

- **NVIDIA Nsight Compute/Systems:**
  Analyze kernel performance, memory throughput, and occupancy.
- **nvprof:**
  A command-line profiler for CUDA applications that provides quick performance metrics.

- **AMD and Intel Tools:**
  Use corresponding profilers for non-NVIDIA hardware to gain similar insights.

Workflow:

1. **Profile Baseline Performance:**
   Run your application with profiling tools to collect baseline metrics.
2. **Identify Bottlenecks:**
   Look for high kernel execution times, low occupancy, or memory access issues.
3. **Implement Changes:**
   Apply optimizations (e.g., kernel fusion, loop unrolling, memory coalescing).
4. **Reprofile:**
   Compare new metrics against baseline performance to gauge improvement.

2. Tuning Kernel Launch Parameters

Concept:
Experiment with different grid and block dimensions to find the optimal configuration:

- **Block Size:**
  The number of threads per block can significantly affect occupancy and performance. Typically, sizes such as 128, 256, or 512 are good starting points.
- **Grid Size:**
  The total number of blocks should be chosen to ensure all GPU cores are effectively utilized.
- **Occupancy Calculator:**
  NVIDIA provides an occupancy calculator that can help estimate the best configuration for your kernel.

3. Memory Hierarchy Optimization

Strategies:

- **Shared Memory:**
  Optimize the use of shared memory by reducing bank conflicts and maximizing data reuse.
- **Cache Utilization:**
  Adjust memory access patterns to improve cache hit rates.
  Techniques like loop tiling and blocking can be very effective.
- **Reduce Global Memory Access:**
  Reuse data already loaded into faster memory types (registers, shared memory) as much as possible.

Code Example: Incorporating Error Checking in CUDA

cpp

```cpp
#include <iostream>
#define CUDA_CHECK(call)                                        \
    do {                                                        \
        cudaError_t error = call;                               \
        if (error != cudaSuccess) {                             \
            std::cerr << "CUDA Error: " <<
cudaGetErrorString(error)                                       \
                        << " at " << __FILE__ << ":" <<
__LINE__ << std::endl;                                          \
            exit(EXIT_FAILURE);                                 \
        }                                                       \
    } while (0)

__global__ void simpleKernel(float *data, int N) {
    int idx = blockIdx.x * blockDim.x + threadIdx.x;
    if (idx < N)
        data[idx] *= 2.0f;
}

int main() {
    int N = 1024;
    size_t size = N * sizeof(float);
    float *h_data = (float *)malloc(size);
    for (int i = 0; i < N; i++) {
        h_data[i] = static_cast<float>(i);
    }

    float *d_data;
```

```
    CUDA_CHECK(cudaMalloc(&d_data, size));
    CUDA_CHECK(cudaMemcpy(d_data, h_data, size,
cudaMemcpyHostToDevice));

    int threadsPerBlock = 256;
    int blocksPerGrid = (N + threadsPerBlock - 1) /
threadsPerBlock;
    simpleKernel<<<blocksPerGrid, threadsPerBlock>>>(d_data,
N);
    CUDA_CHECK(cudaPeekAtLastError());
    CUDA_CHECK(cudaDeviceSynchronize());

    CUDA_CHECK(cudaMemcpy(h_data, d_data, size,
cudaMemcpyDeviceToHost));
    std::cout << "Kernel execution completed successfully."
<< std::endl;

    CUDA_CHECK(cudaFree(d_data));
    free(h_data);
    return 0;
}
```

Explanation:

- The macro CUDA_CHECK wraps CUDA API calls, checking for errors and outputting a message if any occur.
- This practice helps catch issues early during kernel execution and simplifies debugging.

Summary Table: Debugging and Tuning Best Practices

Area	Best Practices	Tools/Techniques
Incremental Development	Develop simple kernels first and gradually add complexity	Unit testing, staged integration
Error Checking & Logging	Check API call returns; log key variables	CUDA_CHECK macros, device logging techniques
Profiling & Analysis	Profile performance regularly to identify bottlenecks	NVIDIA Nsight Compute, nvprof, AMD/Intel profilers

Area	Best Practices	Tools/Techniques
Kernel Tuning	Experiment with grid/block sizes and optimize memory usage	Occupancy calculators, loop unrolling, shared memory optimizations
Asynchronous Execution	Overlap data transfers with computation	CUDA streams, asynchronous memory copies

8.5 Cross-Platform Development and Multi-GPU Systems

As applications grow in complexity and scale, developers increasingly need to leverage the power of multiple GPUs and heterogeneous computing environments. This section examines techniques for cross-platform development and strategies for efficiently utilizing multiple GPUs in a single system.

Cross-Platform Development

Cross-platform development allows applications to run on various hardware and operating systems, maximizing the reach and flexibility of your code. Here are key techniques and tools to achieve cross-platform GPU programming:

1. Abstraction Layers and Frameworks

- **OpenCL:**
  OpenCL (Open Computing Language) is a platform-agnostic framework that supports a wide range of devices including GPUs, CPUs, FPGAs, and DSPs. By writing code in OpenCL, you can target multiple hardware platforms without rewriting your application for each vendor.
  Key Advantages:
    o Vendor neutrality
    o Broad device support
    o Ability to write kernels once and run them on different devices
- **SYCL:**
  SYCL builds on OpenCL to provide a single-source programming

model in modern C++. This simplifies development by combining host and device code in one file and enabling compile-time optimizations using advanced C++ features.

Key Advantages:
- Clean, modern C++ integration
- Single-source development
- Enhanced code portability

- **Vulkan Compute:**
While primarily a graphics API, Vulkan also supports compute operations. Its low-level control over GPU resources and cross-platform support make it attractive for performance-critical applications that need to run on multiple operating systems.

Key Advantages:
- Fine-grained control over hardware
- Reduced driver overhead
- Unified API for graphics and compute

2. Middleware and Libraries

- **Kokkos:**
A C++ library designed for performance portability across various architectures, including GPUs. It abstracts away the hardware details and allows developers to write code that can run on different backends such as CUDA, HIP, and OpenMP.

- **RAJA:**
Developed by Lawrence Livermore National Laboratory, RAJA provides abstractions for parallel loop execution that can target CPUs and GPUs, simplifying the task of writing portable high-performance code.

3. Best Practices for Cross-Platform Development

- **Modular Code Design:**
Write modular and well-abstracted code that separates hardware-specific optimizations from core algorithms. This allows you to swap out or update platform-specific modules without impacting the overall application logic.

- **Conditional Compilation:**
Use preprocessor directives to include or exclude code based on the target platform. This approach helps maintain a single codebase while optimizing for different hardware.

- **Automated Testing and Continuous Integration:**
  Set up automated test suites that run on different platforms and
  devices. Continuous integration (CI) systems can help catch
  platform-specific issues early in the development process.

Multi-GPU Systems and Heterogeneous Computing

When scaling applications across multiple GPUs or combining different
types of processing units (e.g., GPUs, CPUs, and FPGAs), several strategies
come into play:

1. Multi-GPU Programming Models

- **CUDA Multi-GPU Programming:**
  NVIDIA's CUDA provides support for multi-GPU systems.
  Developers can query available GPUs, allocate memory on each
  device, and launch kernels concurrently. Synchronization and data
  sharing between GPUs are managed using features such as CUDA
  streams and peer-to-peer memory access.

  Example Workflow:

  1. **Device Query:** Determine the number of available GPUs.
  2. **Memory Allocation:** Allocate data on each GPU.
  3. **Concurrent Execution:** Launch kernels on multiple GPUs
     concurrently using separate CUDA streams.
  4. **Data Aggregation:** Gather results from all GPUs and
     combine them as needed.
- **MPI with GPUs:**
  Message Passing Interface (MPI) can be combined with GPU
  programming for distributed computing across nodes with multiple
  GPUs. This approach is common in high-performance computing
  (HPC) where tasks are spread across several machines.
- **Unified Memory:**
  Unified memory provides a single memory space accessible by both
  CPUs and GPUs. This can simplify programming by abstracting data
  transfers, although performance tuning is still necessary for optimal
  results.

2. Heterogeneous Computing

- **Task Offloading:**
  Identify parts of your workload that are best suited for different types of processors. For example, CPUs can handle complex control logic and serial tasks, while GPUs perform highly parallel computations.
- **Dynamic Scheduling:**
  Use frameworks that support dynamic task scheduling to distribute workloads among heterogeneous devices based on current load and performance metrics.
- **Interoperability:**
  Ensure that your application efficiently manages data transfers between different devices. Techniques like zero-copy and peer-to-peer memory access can minimize overhead.

Code Example: Simple Multi-GPU Vector Addition Using CUDA

Below is a simplified example demonstrating how to perform vector addition on two GPUs using CUDA. The code initializes two vectors, splits the workload between two GPUs, and then aggregates the results.

```cpp
#include <iostream>
#include <cuda_runtime.h>

#define CUDA_CHECK(call)                                          \
    do {                                                          \
        cudaError_t error = call;                                 \
        if (error != cudaSuccess) {                               \
            std::cerr << "CUDA Error: " <<                        
cudaGetErrorString(error)                           \
                      << " at " << __FILE__ << ":" <<             
__LINE__ << std::endl;          \
            exit(EXIT_FAILURE);                                   
                                                                  \
        }                                                         
                                                                  \
    } while (0)
```

```cpp
__global__ void vectorAdd(const float *A, const float *B,
float *C, int N) {
    int idx = blockIdx.x * blockDim.x + threadIdx.x;
    if (idx < N) {
        C[idx] = A[idx] + B[idx];
    }
}

int main() {
    const int N = 1024;
    size_t size = N * sizeof(float);

    // Allocate host memory
    float *h_A = new float[N];
    float *h_B = new float[N];
    float *h_C = new float[N];

    // Initialize vectors
    for (int i = 0; i < N; i++) {
        h_A[i] = static_cast<float>(i);
        h_B[i] = static_cast<float>(N - i);
    }

    // Query number of GPUs
    int deviceCount;
    CUDA_CHECK(cudaGetDeviceCount(&deviceCount));
    if (deviceCount < 2) {
        std::cerr << "This example requires at least 2 GPUs."
<< std::endl;
        return EXIT_FAILURE;
    }

    // Allocate device memory on GPU 0 and GPU 1 for half of
the vectors
    int halfN = N / 2;
    size_t halfSize = halfN * sizeof(float);
    float *d_A0, *d_B0, *d_C0;
    float *d_A1, *d_B1, *d_C1;

    // GPU 0 allocations
    CUDA_CHECK(cudaSetDevice(0));
    CUDA_CHECK(cudaMalloc(&d_A0, halfSize));
    CUDA_CHECK(cudaMalloc(&d_B0, halfSize));
    CUDA_CHECK(cudaMalloc(&d_C0, halfSize));
    CUDA_CHECK(cudaMemcpy(d_A0, h_A, halfSize,
cudaMemcpyHostToDevice));
    CUDA_CHECK(cudaMemcpy(d_B0, h_B, halfSize,
cudaMemcpyHostToDevice));

    // GPU 1 allocations
    CUDA_CHECK(cudaSetDevice(1));
```

```
    CUDA_CHECK(cudaMalloc(&d_A1, halfSize));
    CUDA_CHECK(cudaMalloc(&d_B1, halfSize));
    CUDA_CHECK(cudaMalloc(&d_C1, halfSize));
    CUDA_CHECK(cudaMemcpy(d_A1, h_A + halfN, halfSize,
cudaMemcpyHostToDevice));
    CUDA_CHECK(cudaMemcpy(d_B1, h_B + halfN, halfSize,
cudaMemcpyHostToDevice));

    // Launch kernels concurrently on both GPUs
    int threadsPerBlock = 256;
    int blocksPerGrid = (halfN + threadsPerBlock - 1) /
threadsPerBlock;

    CUDA_CHECK(cudaSetDevice(0));
    vectorAdd<<<blocksPerGrid, threadsPerBlock>>>(d_A0, d_B0,
d_C0, halfN);
    CUDA_CHECK(cudaSetDevice(1));
    vectorAdd<<<blocksPerGrid, threadsPerBlock>>>(d_A1, d_B1,
d_C1, halfN);

    // Copy results back to host
    CUDA_CHECK(cudaSetDevice(0));
    CUDA_CHECK(cudaMemcpy(h_C, d_C0, halfSize,
cudaMemcpyDeviceToHost));
    CUDA_CHECK(cudaSetDevice(1));
    CUDA_CHECK(cudaMemcpy(h_C + halfN, d_C1, halfSize,
cudaMemcpyDeviceToHost));

    // Verify results (omitted for brevity)
    std::cout << "Multi-GPU vector addition completed." <<
std::endl;

    // Cleanup device memory
    CUDA_CHECK(cudaSetDevice(0));
    cudaFree(d_A0); cudaFree(d_B0); cudaFree(d_C0);
    CUDA_CHECK(cudaSetDevice(1));
    cudaFree(d_A1); cudaFree(d_B1); cudaFree(d_C1);

    // Cleanup host memory
    delete[] h_A;
    delete[] h_B;
    delete[] h_C;

    return 0;
}
```

Explanation:

- **Device Query:** The code first checks for at least two available GPUs.

- **Workload Partitioning:** The vector is split equally between GPU 0 and GPU 1.
- **Concurrent Execution:** Each GPU performs vector addition on its portion of the data.
- **Result Aggregation:** The results from both GPUs are copied back to the host and combined.

8.6 Case Studies: High-Performance GPU Programming in Action

Real-world case studies illustrate how advanced GPU programming techniques are applied in various domains. Here, we highlight examples from both gaming and machine learning to demonstrate high-performance GPU programming.

Case Study 1: Gaming – Real-Time Graphics Rendering

Scenario:
A next-generation gaming engine employs a hybrid rendering pipeline that utilizes both traditional rasterization and real-time ray tracing to achieve photorealistic graphics.

Techniques Employed:

- **Multi-GPU Rendering:**
  The engine distributes rendering tasks across multiple GPUs. One GPU may handle the primary rendering workload while another specializes in real-time ray tracing, ensuring high frame rates and low latency.
- **Optimized Shaders and Compute Kernels:**
  Custom shaders written in GLSL or HLSL are optimized for performance, utilizing advanced techniques such as loop unrolling, shared memory optimization, and asynchronous data transfers.
- **Dynamic Load Balancing:**
  The engine dynamically balances workloads between GPUs based on scene complexity and current performance metrics.

Impact:

- **Frame Rate:**
  Achieves consistently high frame rates (e.g., 60+ FPS) even in graphically complex scenes.
- **Visual Quality:**
  Delivers lifelike lighting, shadows, and reflections through efficient real-time ray tracing.
- **User Experience:**
  Provides a smooth and immersive gaming experience without noticeable performance hitches.

Case Study 2: Machine Learning – Distributed Deep Learning Training

Scenario:
Training a large-scale deep neural network, such as a transformer model for natural language processing, on a distributed system of multiple GPUs.

Techniques Employed:

- **Data Parallelism and Model Parallelism:**
  The training workload is distributed across several GPUs. Data parallelism splits the mini-batches across GPUs, while model parallelism divides the network layers among devices.
- **Efficient Communication:**
  Techniques like NVIDIA's NCCL (NVIDIA Collective Communications Library) are used to synchronize gradients and parameters efficiently across GPUs.
- **Mixed-Precision Training:**
  To reduce memory usage and accelerate computation, mixed-precision training is implemented using libraries like NVIDIA's Apex or PyTorch's native support.

Impact:

- **Training Time:**
  Significantly reduced training time, from weeks to days, by leveraging the full computational power of the multi-GPU setup.
- **Scalability:**
  The system scales efficiently with the addition of more GPUs, allowing for training even larger models.

- **Cost Efficiency:**
  Optimizations reduce power consumption and hardware costs while maintaining high performance.

Summary Table: Case Studies Overview

Domain	Application	Techniques Employed	Key Benefits
Gaming	Real-Time Graphics Rendering	Multi-GPU rendering, optimized shaders, dynamic load balancing	High frame rates, photorealistic visuals, immersive gameplay
Machine Learning	Distributed Deep Learning Training	Data/model parallelism, efficient inter-GPU communication (NCCL), mixed-precision training	Reduced training time, scalable performance, cost and energy efficiency

Chapter Summary

In Chapter 8, we explored advanced programming and development techniques for GPU architectures, focusing on cross-platform development and the efficient use of multi-GPU systems. Section 8.5 discussed strategies for cross-platform development, including the use of abstraction layers such as OpenCL, SYCL, and Vulkan Compute, as well as best practices for modular code design and conditional compilation. We also examined techniques for multi-GPU programming, demonstrating how to partition workloads and manage data across GPUs in a heterogeneous environment with a detailed CUDA example.

Chapter 9: The Future of GPU Technology

The landscape of GPU technology continues to evolve at a rapid pace, driven by relentless innovation in hardware design, manufacturing techniques, and the ever-expanding demands of modern applications. In this chapter, we explore the future of GPU technology, focusing on next-generation architectures and the impact of emerging technologies such as IoT, edge computing, and quantum acceleration.

9.1 Next-Generation Architectures and Innovations on the Horizon

Overview

Next-generation GPUs are poised to push the boundaries of performance, energy efficiency, and versatility. Innovations in semiconductor manufacturing, architectural design, and specialized hardware integration are shaping the future of GPU design. These advancements will not only enhance traditional graphics processing but also revolutionize general-purpose computation, artificial intelligence, and high-performance computing.

Key Areas of Innovation

1. Increased Core Density and Heterogeneous Architectures

- **Core Density:**
  As manufacturing processes continue to shrink, future GPUs will feature even higher densities of processing cores. This increase will allow for massive parallelism, enabling more complex and data-intensive computations.
- **Heterogeneous Integration:**
  Next-generation GPUs are expected to integrate multiple types of specialized cores—such as enhanced tensor cores, ray tracing cores, and AI accelerators—within a single chip. This heterogeneous architecture will allow GPUs to dynamically allocate resources based

on the workload, optimizing performance and efficiency across different applications.

2. Advanced Memory Systems

- **Next-Generation High-Bandwidth Memory (HBM):**
  Future GPUs will likely adopt newer versions of HBM or similar memory technologies that offer even greater bandwidth and lower latency. These advances are critical for handling the enormous data volumes used in deep learning, scientific simulations, and real-time rendering.
- **On-Chip Memory Enhancements:**
  Innovations in cache design and shared memory will further reduce data access latency. Techniques such as adaptive caching and intelligent prefetching may become standard, ensuring that data is always available where it is needed most.

3. Energy Efficiency and Thermal Management

- **Dynamic Power Management:**
  Future GPUs will incorporate more sophisticated dynamic voltage and frequency scaling (DVFS) and power gating mechanisms to optimize energy consumption in real time. This is especially important as applications demand higher performance while operating within power and thermal constraints.
- **Advanced Cooling Solutions:**
  To manage increased power densities, next-generation GPUs will leverage innovative cooling techniques. These may include integrated liquid cooling, advanced heat sink designs, and novel materials that improve thermal conductivity.

4. Software and Programming Model Innovations

- **Unified Development Frameworks:**
  As hardware becomes more complex, software frameworks will evolve to provide a unified programming model that abstracts the underlying heterogeneity. This will make it easier for developers to write code that efficiently utilizes all available processing units.
- **Machine Learning Integration:**
  With the rise of AI, future GPU architectures will be designed with native support for deep learning workloads. This includes further

enhancements to tensor processing units and dedicated hardware for common neural network operations.

Future Architectural Roadmap Summary

Aspect	Current Trends	Future Innovations
Core Density & Heterogeneity	Thousands of cores with specialized units (e.g., tensor, ray tracing cores)	Even higher core density; integration of diverse specialized cores for dynamic resource allocation
Memory Systems	High-Bandwidth Memory (HBM), multi-level caches	Next-gen HBM with increased bandwidth, adaptive caching, and lower latency on-chip memory systems
Energy Efficiency	Dynamic power management, basic DVFS	Advanced DVFS, power gating, and integrated thermal management; improved cooling solutions
Software Ecosystem	CUDA, OpenCL, Vulkan, proprietary AI libraries	Unified, cross-platform development frameworks; deeper integration with AI and automated optimization tools

Example Scenario: Future GPU in a Deep Learning Data Center

Imagine a data center equipped with next-generation GPUs featuring a heterogeneous architecture with thousands of cores. These GPUs integrate enhanced tensor cores for deep learning, along with traditional shader and ray tracing cores for data visualization and simulation. Advanced HBM ensures rapid data access, while dynamic power management and innovative cooling maintain energy efficiency. A unified software framework enables researchers to develop and deploy complex neural network models without worrying about the underlying hardware specifics, dramatically reducing training times and energy costs.

9.2 The Impact of Emerging Technologies: IoT, Edge Computing, and Quantum Acceleration

Overview

Emerging technologies such as the Internet of Things (IoT), edge computing, and quantum acceleration are poised to significantly influence GPU development. As computing moves closer to the data source and new paradigms emerge, GPUs must adapt to meet the changing requirements of these fields.

1. IoT and Edge Computing

Edge Computing

- **Concept:**
  Edge computing involves processing data near its source rather than relying solely on centralized data centers. This reduces latency, improves responsiveness, and conserves bandwidth.
- **GPU Role:**
  Future GPUs designed for edge computing will be optimized for low power consumption and compact form factors while maintaining high computational capabilities. They will enable real-time analytics, object recognition, and decision-making in IoT devices.
- **Impact:**
  Applications such as autonomous vehicles, smart cameras, and industrial IoT systems will benefit from accelerated local processing, reducing the need for constant cloud connectivity.

IoT Integration

- **Scalability:**
  The proliferation of IoT devices generates vast amounts of data that require real-time processing. GPUs with energy-efficient architectures will be integral in handling these data streams, performing complex computations on the fly.
- **Interoperability:**
  Future GPUs will likely offer enhanced support for diverse communication protocols and interfaces to seamlessly integrate with various IoT platforms and sensors.

2. Quantum Acceleration

Quantum Computing Integration

- **Concept:**
  Quantum computing represents a fundamentally different approach to computation, leveraging quantum bits (qubits) to solve certain classes of problems exponentially faster than classical computers.
- **Hybrid Systems:**
  While full-scale quantum computers are still in development, hybrid systems that combine classical GPUs with quantum co-processors are emerging. These systems use GPUs to handle classical processing tasks while delegating specific, computation-intensive problems to quantum processors.
- **Potential Applications:**
  Fields such as cryptography, complex system simulations, and optimization problems could see significant breakthroughs through the integration of quantum acceleration with GPU computing.
- **Challenges:**
  Integrating quantum processors with classical GPUs requires the development of new programming models and communication protocols to manage data exchange and synchronization between the two computing paradigms.

3. Convergence of Emerging Technologies

Unified Platforms

- **Interdisciplinary Platforms:**
  Future computing platforms may integrate IoT, edge, and quantum technologies into a cohesive system. GPUs will serve as the backbone for classical processing while interfacing with specialized accelerators.
- **Software Ecosystem:**
  Developers will need new tools and frameworks that abstract the complexities of these heterogeneous systems, allowing them to focus on application logic rather than hardware integration details.

Future Directions Summary Table

Emerging Technology	Description	Impact on GPU Development
IoT and Edge Computing	Processing data close to the source, enabling low-latency, real-time applications	Development of energy-efficient, compact GPUs with high-performance capabilities for real-time analytics
Quantum Acceleration	Integration of quantum processors to handle specific, complex computations	Hybrid systems combining classical and quantum computing; new programming models and communication protocols
Unified Platforms	Convergence of IoT, edge, and quantum technologies into cohesive systems	Cross-disciplinary development frameworks; enhanced interoperability and scalability

Example Scenario: Smart City Infrastructure

Consider a smart city infrastructure where IoT sensors continuously monitor traffic, environmental conditions, and public safety. Edge devices equipped with compact, energy-efficient GPUs perform real-time data analytics to manage traffic flow and detect anomalies. For more complex tasks such as optimizing energy distribution or running large-scale simulations of urban dynamics, the data is transmitted to regional centers where hybrid systems combine classical GPU processing with quantum accelerators. Unified software frameworks enable seamless integration, ensuring that decision-making is both rapid and precise.

9.3 Sustainable and Energy-Efficient GPU Designs

As computational demands continue to rise across various domains, the energy consumption and environmental impact of high-performance computing systems have become critical concerns. Sustainable and energy-efficient GPU designs aim to deliver high performance while minimizing power usage, reducing thermal output, and ultimately lowering the carbon footprint. In this section, we explore the strategies and innovations driving sustainable GPU design.

Key Strategies for Energy Efficiency

1. Dynamic Voltage and Frequency Scaling (DVFS)

- **Concept:**
  DVFS adjusts the voltage and operating frequency of GPU components dynamically based on workload demands.
- **Benefits:**
  - **Lower Power Consumption:** When the workload is light, the GPU operates at reduced frequencies and voltages, saving energy.
  - **Thermal Management:** Reduced operating frequencies help lower the heat generated, minimizing the need for aggressive cooling solutions.
- **Implementation:**
  Many modern GPUs incorporate built-in DVFS mechanisms that are managed by firmware and drivers. These adjustments are often transparent to the application developer.

2. Power Gating and Clock Gating

- **Power Gating:**
  - **Concept:** Portions of the GPU that are idle are temporarily powered down to save energy.
  - **Impact:** By shutting off power to unused units, overall energy consumption is reduced without compromising performance during peak operations.
- **Clock Gating:**
  - **Concept:** Stops the clock signal to inactive circuits while keeping them in a ready state.
  - **Impact:** Reduces dynamic power consumption by lowering the switching activity within the chip.

3. Advanced Semiconductor Processes

- **Smaller Process Nodes:**
  - **Concept:** The transition to smaller process nodes (e.g., 7nm, 5nm) allows for more transistors to be packed into a given area with lower power consumption per transistor.

- Impact: This increased transistor density can lead to higher performance and lower power consumption, thanks to reduced leakage currents and improved energy efficiency.
- **New Materials and Transistor Architectures:**
  - **Examples:** FinFET and Gate-All-Around (GAA) transistors provide better control over current flow, reduce leakage, and improve overall performance per watt.

4. Thermal-Aware Design and Advanced Cooling

- **Thermal Management:**
  - **Techniques:** Integration of advanced cooling systems such as vapor chambers, liquid cooling, and innovative heat spreaders to efficiently dissipate heat.
  - **Impact:** Better thermal management allows GPUs to maintain higher performance levels without throttling and reduces the need for high-power cooling solutions.
- **Design for Low Thermal Density:**
  - **Approach:** Optimizing the layout and packaging of GPU components to minimize hotspots and distribute heat more evenly across the chip.

5. Software-Level Optimizations

- **Efficient Kernel Design:**
  - **Concept:** Writing optimized code that minimizes idle cycles and maximizes resource utilization can reduce unnecessary power consumption.
- **Energy-Aware Scheduling:**
  - **Techniques:** Operating systems and GPU drivers can schedule tasks to optimize energy efficiency, such as bundling workloads to avoid frequent power state transitions.

Summary Table: Energy Efficiency Techniques in GPUs

Technique	Description	Benefits
Dynamic Voltage & Frequency Scaling (DVFS)	Adjusts voltage and frequency based on workload demand	Reduced power consumption and lower thermal output

Technique	Description	Benefits
Power Gating	Shuts down idle GPU components	Saves energy by reducing leakage and dynamic power usage
Clock Gating	Stops the clock signal to inactive circuits	Minimizes switching power, enhancing overall energy efficiency
Advanced Semiconductor Processes	Use of smaller process nodes and new materials (e.g., FinFET, GAA)	Higher transistor density with lower power consumption per transistor
Advanced Cooling Solutions	Innovative cooling methods (liquid cooling, vapor chambers)	Efficient heat dissipation, improved performance stability
Software-Level Optimizations	Efficient kernel design and energy-aware scheduling	Lowered computational waste, optimized power usage throughout execution

9.4 GPUs in Exascale and High-Performance Computing (HPC)

The march toward exascale computing—systems capable of performing at least one exaFLOP (10^{18} floating-point operations per second)—is reshaping the high-performance computing (HPC) landscape. GPUs play a pivotal role in this transformation, providing the massive parallelism and energy efficiency required for next-generation supercomputers.

The Role of GPUs in Exascale Computing

1. Unprecedented Parallelism

- **Massive Throughput:**
  GPUs offer thousands of parallel processing cores, enabling them to tackle the immense computational demands of exascale applications such as climate modeling, genomics, and advanced physics simulations.
- **Scalable Architectures:**
  Modern GPUs are designed to work in multi-GPU and multi-node

configurations, ensuring that computational tasks can be distributed efficiently across large clusters.

2. Energy Efficiency at Scale

- **Power Constraints:**
  Exascale systems must operate within strict power budgets, often in the range of 20-30 megawatts for an entire supercomputer.
- **Efficient Designs:**
  Energy-efficient GPU designs (as discussed in Section 9.3) are crucial for meeting these power constraints while delivering exascale-level performance.

3. Advanced Interconnects and Memory Architectures

- **High-Speed Interconnects:**
  Technologies such as NVIDIA's NVLink and AMD's Infinity Fabric, along with emerging standards like PCIe 5.0/6.0, enable rapid communication between GPUs, as well as between GPUs and CPUs. These interconnects are essential for scaling up performance in multi-GPU systems.
- **Unified Memory Architectures:**
  Unified memory systems help in minimizing data transfer bottlenecks, enabling smoother scaling across nodes and reducing latency in memory-intensive operations.

4. Software and Programming Models

- **Optimized Libraries and Frameworks:**
  Libraries such as cuDNN, cuBLAS, and NCCL (for NVIDIA GPUs) are integral to achieving high performance in exascale environments. These libraries are optimized for multi-GPU setups and provide the building blocks for complex simulations.
- **HPC-Specific APIs:**
  APIs like MPI (Message Passing Interface) combined with GPU programming models allow for efficient parallel processing across distributed systems.

Future Exascale Systems: A Glimpse

Consider a future exascale supercomputer comprising tens of thousands of nodes, each equipped with multiple GPUs optimized for both compute performance and energy efficiency. Such systems will be capable of running highly complex simulations in near real-time, with applications ranging from weather forecasting to drug discovery.

Summary Table: GPUs in Exascale and HPC

Aspect	Role in Exascale/HPC	Key Requirements
Parallelism	Enable massive concurrent computations	Thousands of cores, scalable multi-GPU architectures
Energy Efficiency	Maintain performance within strict power budgets	Low-power designs, advanced DVFS, power gating
Interconnects	Facilitate rapid communication between GPUs and nodes	High-speed interconnects (NVLink, PCIe 5.0/6.0, Infinity Fabric)
Memory Architectures	Reduce data transfer bottlenecks	Unified memory, high-bandwidth memory (HBM)
Software Ecosystem	Provide optimized libraries and APIs for HPC workloads	HPC-specific libraries (cuDNN, NCCL) and MPI integration

9.5 Visionary Predictions and Research Directions

Looking toward the future, GPU technology is poised to enter a new era marked by radical innovations and transformative applications. In this section, we present expert insights and predictions on where GPU technology is headed, along with promising research directions.

Emerging Trends and Research Directions

1. Integration with Artificial Intelligence

- **AI-Optimized Architectures:**
  GPUs will continue to evolve with a tighter integration of AI-specific hardware, such as more advanced tensor cores and dedicated AI accelerators.
- **Unified AI Systems:**
  The convergence of AI algorithms and GPU hardware may lead to systems where machine learning processes are deeply embedded in the GPU architecture, enabling real-time, on-device AI applications.

2. Quantum and Neuromorphic Computing

- **Hybrid Systems:**
  As quantum computing matures, we can anticipate hybrid systems that combine classical GPU processing with quantum accelerators for specific problem domains, such as optimization and cryptography.
- **Neuromorphic Architectures:**
  Inspired by the human brain, neuromorphic chips mimic neural structures and can operate at extremely low power. These architectures could complement or, in some cases, replace traditional GPUs for certain types of AI tasks.

3. Edge and Distributed Computing

- **Edge GPUs:**
  With the expansion of IoT and edge computing, there is a growing need for compact, energy-efficient GPUs that can operate at the network edge. These GPUs will empower real-time analytics and decision-making in applications such as autonomous vehicles and smart cities.
- **Distributed AI Systems:**
  Future systems may distribute AI workloads across a network of edge devices and centralized data centers, requiring sophisticated coordination and data synchronization protocols.

4. Advancements in Materials and Manufacturing

- **Next-Generation Semiconductors:**
  The continuous push for smaller process nodes and novel materials (such as graphene and other 2D materials) will further enhance GPU performance and energy efficiency.

- **3D Integration and Packaging:**
  Future GPUs may leverage advanced 3D stacking and heterogeneous integration techniques to achieve even higher levels of performance within a smaller footprint.

Expert Predictions

- **Performance Gains:**
  Experts predict that next-generation GPUs could deliver performance improvements of 2-3 times per generation, driven by both architectural innovations and process node advancements.
- **Energy Efficiency:**
  The industry is expected to achieve significant gains in energy efficiency, potentially reducing power consumption per operation by up to 50% through advanced power management and cooling technologies.
- **AI and HPC Convergence:**
  As AI applications become increasingly complex, the line between traditional HPC and AI-specific computing will continue to blur, leading to unified systems optimized for both domains.

Visionary Research Directions

Research Area	Focus	Potential Impact
Hybrid Quantum-Classical Systems	Integration of quantum processors with classical GPUs	Solving complex optimization and simulation problems more efficiently
Neuromorphic Computing	Bio-inspired architectures for ultra-low-power AI processing	Enabling energy-efficient, real-time processing for sensory and pattern recognition tasks
Edge AI GPUs	Compact, low-power GPUs designed for the network edge	Expanding AI capabilities to remote and mobile applications, reducing reliance on centralized data centers
Advanced Materials & 3D Integration	Use of novel semiconductor materials and 3D stacking for	Increased performance in a smaller form factor, improved thermal

Research Area	Focus	Potential Impact
	higher density and efficiency	management and energy efficiency

Chapter Summary

In Chapter 9, we explored the future of GPU technology, focusing on the next generation of architectures and the impact of emerging technological trends. Section 9.1 provided an in-depth look at upcoming innovations, including increased core density, heterogeneous architectures, advanced memory systems, and improved energy efficiency. We discussed how these developments will drive significant performance gains and support a wide range of applications from AI to HPC.

Appendices and Supplementary Materials

The final chapter of this book is designed to serve as a comprehensive resource for readers seeking additional context, definitions, and further materials to deepen their understanding of GPU technology. In this chapter, you will find a detailed glossary of technical terms and acronyms, as well as a curated list of further reading and recommended resources, including books, research papers, and online materials.

10.1 Glossary of Terms and Acronyms

This glossary provides clear and concise definitions for the technical terms, abbreviations, and acronyms used throughout the book. It is intended as a quick reference guide to help you understand the language and concepts of GPU architecture, programming, and optimization.

A

- **API (Application Programming Interface):**
  A set of routines, protocols, and tools for building software applications. In the context of GPUs, APIs such as CUDA, OpenCL, Vulkan, and DirectCompute provide the means to program and utilize GPU hardware.
- **ASIC (Application-Specific Integrated Circuit):**
  A microchip designed for a particular application or purpose, as opposed to a general-purpose processor. GPUs are a form of ASIC specialized for graphics and parallel computation.

B

- **Bandwidth:**
  The maximum rate at which data can be transferred over a network or between components, typically measured in gigabytes per second (GB/s). In GPUs, memory bandwidth is a critical parameter that affects data transfer speeds between the GPU and its memory.

C

- **CUDA (Compute Unified Device Architecture):**
  A parallel computing platform and programming model developed by NVIDIA that allows developers to use NVIDIA GPUs for general-purpose processing. CUDA extends C/C++ with language constructs to define parallel kernels.
- **Compute Kernel:**
  A function or routine that runs on the GPU and is executed in parallel by many threads. Kernels are the core units of computation in GPU programming.
- **Core:**
  The basic processing unit of a GPU. Modern GPUs consist of hundreds or thousands of cores that work concurrently to execute parallel operations.

D

- **DirectCompute:**
  A Microsoft API that allows the use of GPU resources for general-purpose computing tasks within the DirectX ecosystem, primarily on Windows platforms.

E

- **Energy Efficiency:**
  A measure of how effectively a GPU converts electrical power into computational work. Energy-efficient designs reduce power consumption and heat generation, which is crucial for sustainable computing and data centers.

F

- **FLOPS (Floating Point Operations Per Second):**
  A metric for measuring computational performance, especially in scientific and graphics applications. It indicates how many floating-point calculations a GPU or CPU can perform per second.

G

- **GPU (Graphics Processing Unit):**
  A specialized processor designed for rendering images and performing parallel computations. Modern GPUs are widely used in gaming, machine learning, high-performance computing (HPC), and other data-intensive applications.
- **GDDR (Graphics Double Data Rate):**
  A type of memory specifically designed for graphics applications, offering high bandwidth and optimized for fast data access.

H

- **HBM (High-Bandwidth Memory):**
  An advanced type of memory that provides significantly higher bandwidth and lower power consumption compared to traditional GDDR memory. HBM is used in high-end GPUs to enhance data throughput.

I

- **IoT (Internet of Things):**
  A network of interconnected devices embedded with sensors and software that collect and exchange data. In the context of GPU technology, IoT devices may utilize energy-efficient GPUs for edge computing and real-time analytics.

K

- **Kernel:**
  In GPU programming, a kernel is a function executed on the GPU that runs concurrently across multiple data elements. Kernels are launched from the host and are the primary units of parallel execution.

L

- **Latency:**
  The delay between initiating an operation and its completion. In GPU applications, low latency is crucial for real-time processing tasks.

M

- **Memory Coalescing:**
  A technique used to combine multiple memory accesses into a single, efficient transaction. Coalescing is important for maximizing memory throughput on GPUs.
- **Multi-GPU:**
  A system configuration where two or more GPUs are used concurrently to improve performance. Multi-GPU programming involves distributing workloads and managing data transfers between GPUs.

N

- **NVIDIA:**
  A leading manufacturer of GPUs and the developer of CUDA. NVIDIA's GPU architectures (e.g., GeForce, Tesla, and Quadro series) have driven significant advancements in graphics and parallel computing.
- **Nsight:**
  A suite of performance analysis and debugging tools developed by NVIDIA. Nsight Systems and Nsight Compute are commonly used for profiling GPU applications.

O

- **OpenCL (Open Computing Language):**
  An open standard for cross-platform, parallel programming that supports a variety of devices, including GPUs, CPUs, and FPGAs. OpenCL provides a vendor-neutral API for heterogeneous computing.

P

- **Power Gating:**
  A technique used to shut down inactive parts of a GPU to reduce power consumption. Power gating is essential for energy-efficient design.
- **Performance Optimization:**
  The process of improving the efficiency and speed of GPU-based applications through various techniques such as kernel fusion, memory optimization, and tuning of execution parameters.

Q

- **Quantum Acceleration:**
  The integration of quantum processors with classical GPUs to solve specific computational problems more efficiently. This emerging field explores hybrid systems that leverage both quantum and classical computing.

R

- **Rasterization:**
  The process of converting vector graphics (shapes, lines) into a raster image (pixels). Traditional GPU graphics pipelines rely on rasterization, while modern techniques also include ray tracing.

S

- **Shader:**
  A program executed on the GPU to perform rendering operations. Shaders can be used for vertex processing, pixel processing, and other effects in graphics applications.
- **SIMT (Single Instruction, Multiple Threads):**
  An execution model where a single instruction is executed across multiple threads concurrently. This model is fundamental to GPU architectures, enabling massive parallelism.
- **SYCL:**
  A high-level programming model built on OpenCL that allows single-source C++ programming for heterogeneous computing. SYCL simplifies the development of portable, cross-platform GPU applications.

T

- **Tensor Core:**
  A specialized processing unit found in modern NVIDIA GPUs designed to accelerate matrix operations commonly used in deep learning. Tensor cores enable significant performance improvements for neural network training and inference.
- **Throughput:**
  The rate at which a system can process data, typically measured in

operations per second or data transferred per second. High throughput is a key indicator of GPU performance.

U

- **Unified Memory:**
  A memory management system that provides a single address space accessible by both the CPU and GPU, simplifying data transfers and reducing programming complexity.

V

- **Vulkan:**
  A low-level, cross-platform API for graphics and compute that provides explicit control over GPU resources. Vulkan is known for its efficiency and reduced driver overhead.

W

- **Warp:**
  A group of threads (typically 32 in NVIDIA GPUs) that execute in lockstep on a GPU. The concept of warps is fundamental to understanding GPU execution and optimization strategies.

Z

- **Zero-Copy:**
  A technique that allows the GPU to directly access host memory without the need for an explicit data copy, reducing latency and improving performance in certain applications.

10.2 Further Reading and Recommended Resources

This section provides a curated list of additional resources to help you delve deeper into GPU technology, programming, and performance optimization. Whether you are a beginner or an advanced developer, the following books, research papers, online courses, and websites offer valuable insights and practical knowledge.

Books

1. **"Programming Massively Parallel Processors: A Hands-on Approach" by David B. Kirk and Wen-mei W. Hwu**
   o A comprehensive guide to GPU programming using CUDA. It covers fundamentals, optimization techniques, and advanced topics, making it a great resource for both beginners and experienced developers.
2. **"CUDA by Example: An Introduction to General-Purpose GPU Programming" by Jason Sanders and Edward Kandrot**
   o This book provides practical examples and step-by-step tutorials for writing CUDA applications. It's an excellent starting point for developers new to GPU programming.
3. **"GPU Pro/GPU Zen Series" (various authors)**
   o A series of books that delve into advanced graphics programming techniques, including real-time rendering, ray tracing, and performance optimization. These books are ideal for game developers and graphics programmers.
4. **"Heterogeneous Computing with OpenCL 2.0" by David R. Kaeli, Perhaad Mistry, Dana Schaa, and Dong Ping Zhang**
   o A detailed look at OpenCL, offering insights into programming heterogeneous systems that include GPUs, CPUs, and other accelerators.

Research Papers

1. **"A Survey of General-Purpose Computation on Graphics Hardware"**
   o Provides an overview of early and current trends in GPU computing. It's a foundational paper that discusses the evolution of GPUs from graphics accelerators to general-purpose processors.
2. **"The Landscape of Parallel Computing Research: A View from Berkeley"**
   o This paper outlines future directions and challenges in parallel computing, including GPU advancements. It's useful for understanding the broader context of GPU research.
3. **Recent conference proceedings from venues such as SIGGRAPH, SC (Supercomputing Conference), and ISC High Performance**

- These conferences publish cutting-edge research on GPU architectures, performance optimization, and emerging applications in AI and HPC.

Online Resources and Courses

1. **NVIDIA Developer Zone (https://developer.nvidia.com/)**
   - A hub for all things related to NVIDIA GPU development, including documentation, tutorials, SDKs, and forums.
2. **Khronos Group (https://www.khronos.org/)**
   - The organization behind OpenCL, Vulkan, and SYCL. Their website offers specifications, tutorials, and resources for learning these APIs.
3. **Coursera and Udacity Courses on GPU Programming and Parallel Computing**
   - Many online courses provide in-depth training in CUDA programming, parallel computing, and GPU optimization. Look for courses such as "Intro to Parallel Programming with CUDA" on Udacity or related offerings on Coursera.
4. **YouTube Channels and Technical Blogs:**
   - Channels like NVIDIA's official YouTube channel, and technical blogs from companies like AMD and Intel, offer webinars, tutorials, and discussions on the latest GPU innovations and best practices.

Online Communities and Forums

1. **Stack Overflow:**
   - An excellent resource for troubleshooting and discussing GPU programming challenges. You can find threads on CUDA, OpenCL, Vulkan, and more.
2. **Reddit Communities:**
   - Subreddits such as r/gpu, r/cuda, and r/parallelcomputing are active forums where professionals share insights, ask questions, and discuss the latest trends in GPU technology.
3. **GitHub:**
   - Explore open-source projects and libraries related to GPU computing. Repositories can serve as practical examples of advanced techniques and optimization strategies.

Summary Table: Recommended Resources

Resource Type	Examples	Description
Books	"Programming Massively Parallel Processors", "CUDA by Example", "GPU Pro/GPU Zen", "Heterogeneous Computing with OpenCL 2.0"	In-depth guides on GPU programming, optimization, and graphics rendering.
Research Papers	"A Survey of General-Purpose Computation on Graphics Hardware", "The Landscape of Parallel Computing Research"	Foundational and advanced papers that provide insights into GPU evolution.
Online Courses	Udacity's "Intro to Parallel Programming with CUDA", Coursera GPU programming courses	Interactive courses offering practical training in GPU and parallel computing.
Websites/Communities	NVIDIA Developer Zone, Khronos Group, Stack Overflow, Reddit, GitHub	Platforms for documentation, tutorials, community support, and open-source projects.

10.3 Tools and Software for GPU Development

A robust ecosystem of tools, libraries, and simulators is essential for developing, debugging, and optimizing GPU applications. This section provides an in-depth overview of the key development tools available to GPU programmers, ranging from low-level profilers to high-level libraries and simulators. These tools enable developers to write efficient code, diagnose performance bottlenecks, and simulate GPU behavior before deployment.

Development Tools

1. Compilers and Programming Environments

- **NVIDIA CUDA Compiler (nvcc):**
  The primary compiler for CUDA C/C++ code, nvcc compiles kernels and host code to produce binaries optimized for NVIDIA GPUs. It supports various optimization flags, debugging symbols, and can target different compute capabilities.
- **Clang/LLVM for OpenCL and SYCL:**
  The LLVM project, along with Clang, provides support for compiling OpenCL and SYCL code. These compilers enable cross-platform development and optimization by generating intermediate representations that can be further optimized for specific hardware.
- **Vulkan SDK:**
  The Vulkan Software Development Kit includes compilers, libraries, and debugging tools for developing both graphics and compute applications using Vulkan. It is designed for low-level control and high efficiency, supporting multiple platforms.

2. Libraries and Frameworks

- **cuDNN, cuBLAS, and cuFFT:**
  These are specialized NVIDIA libraries for deep learning, basic linear algebra operations, and Fast Fourier Transforms, respectively. They are highly optimized for NVIDIA GPUs and serve as critical building blocks for machine learning frameworks.
- **Thrust:**
  A C++ template library for CUDA that provides high-level abstractions for parallel algorithms and data structures. Thrust is similar to the C++ Standard Template Library (STL) and allows for rapid development of GPU-accelerated applications with minimal code changes.
- **OpenCL Libraries:**
  Many vendors provide OpenCL libraries that support a wide range of devices. These libraries facilitate the development of portable applications that can run on GPUs, CPUs, and other accelerators.
- **Vulkan and DirectX:**
  For graphics-intensive applications, Vulkan and DirectX (including DirectCompute) offer APIs that allow for low-level GPU control and efficient management of graphics and compute workloads.

3. Profiling and Debugging Tools

- **NVIDIA Nsight Systems and Nsight Compute:**
  Nsight Systems provides a system-wide view of CPU-GPU interactions, while Nsight Compute offers detailed, kernel-level performance metrics such as memory throughput, occupancy, and latency. Both tools are invaluable for identifying bottlenecks and optimizing performance.
- **CUDA-GDB:**
  A debugging tool specifically designed for CUDA applications. It allows developers to step through GPU code, inspect variables, and diagnose errors in parallel execution.
- **AMD Radeon GPU Profiler (RGP):**
  For AMD GPUs, RGP provides similar profiling capabilities to NVIDIA's tools, offering insights into shader performance, memory usage, and pipeline efficiency.
- **Intel Graphics Performance Analyzers (GPA):**
  Intel GPA is used for profiling and debugging GPU applications on Intel hardware, providing real-time performance data and optimization recommendations.

4. Simulators and Emulators

- **GPGPU-Sim:**
  An open-source simulator that models modern GPU architectures at a detailed level. GPGPU-Sim is widely used in academic research to evaluate new architectural ideas and optimizations before hardware is built.
- **Multi2Sim:**
  A simulation framework that supports both CPU and GPU architectures, enabling the study of heterogeneous computing systems. Multi2Sim provides a versatile environment for simulating complex interactions between different processing units.
- **Oclgrind:**
  An OpenCL device simulator that helps developers debug OpenCL code without requiring access to physical hardware. Oclgrind simulates the execution of OpenCL kernels, making it easier to identify issues like race conditions or memory access violations.

Summary Table: Essential Tools and Software for GPU Development

Category	Tools/Software	Key Functions
Compilers	nvcc, Clang/LLVM, Vulkan SDK	Compiling GPU code for NVIDIA, OpenCL/SYCL, Vulkan
Libraries	cuDNN, cuBLAS, cuFFT, Thrust, OpenCL libraries, Vulkan, DirectX	Providing optimized routines for deep learning, linear algebra, FFTs, and graphics/compute workloads
Profiling & Debugging	NVIDIA Nsight Systems/Compute, CUDA-GDB, AMD RGP, Intel GPA	Performance analysis, debugging, memory usage optimization, occupancy measurement
Simulators/Emulators	GPGPU-Sim, Multi2Sim, Oclgrind	Simulating GPU architectures, debugging OpenCL code, modeling heterogeneous systems

10.4 Interactive Online Resources and Tutorials

In addition to traditional development tools, numerous online resources offer interactive tutorials, video lectures, code repositories, and community forums that can help you master GPU development. These resources provide hands-on learning experiences and keep you updated with the latest trends and best practices in the field.

1. Video Lectures and Online Courses

- **NVIDIA Developer YouTube Channel:**
  Offers a wide range of tutorials, webinars, and recorded sessions on CUDA programming, GPU architecture, and deep learning optimization techniques.
- **Udacity's "Intro to Parallel Programming with CUDA":**
  An online course that provides a thorough introduction to GPU

programming with CUDA. It covers the fundamentals of parallel programming, kernel optimization, and real-world applications.

- **Coursera and edX Courses:**
  Many universities and institutions offer courses on parallel computing and GPU programming. Look for courses on platforms such as Coursera (e.g., "GPU Programming and Architecture") and edX that provide structured learning paths.

2. Code Repositories and Interactive Platforms

- **GitHub:**
  GitHub is a rich resource for open-source projects and sample code related to GPU development. Many repositories offer complete examples of CUDA, OpenCL, and Vulkan applications, along with documentation and community support.
- **CUDA Samples:**
  NVIDIA provides a repository of CUDA samples that demonstrate various aspects of GPU programming—from basic vector operations to advanced deep learning kernels. These samples are an excellent starting point for new projects.
- **Kaggle:**
  For those interested in GPU-accelerated machine learning, Kaggle offers numerous datasets and notebooks that demonstrate the use of GPUs in training models. Many notebooks include optimized code examples and performance benchmarks.
- **Interactive Tutorials:**
  Websites like **LearnCUDA.com** and **OpenCLTutorials.com** offer interactive, browser-based tutorials that guide you through the basics of GPU programming. These platforms often include live coding environments and challenges to reinforce learning.

3. Forums and Community Platforms

- **Stack Overflow:**
  A popular forum where developers can ask questions, share knowledge, and troubleshoot issues related to GPU programming. Tags such as "CUDA," "OpenCL," and "Vulkan" provide access to a wealth of community expertise.
- **Reddit:**
  Subreddits like r/gpu, r/cuda, and r/parallelcomputing are active communities where enthusiasts and professionals discuss the latest trends, share projects, and offer advice on GPU development.

- **NVIDIA Developer Forums:**
  NVIDIA's official forums provide a platform for discussing CUDA, GPU architectures, and performance optimization. Here, developers can interact directly with NVIDIA engineers and other experienced professionals.

Summary Table: Interactive Online Resources and Tutorials

Resource Type	Examples/Platforms	Content/Features
Video Lectures/Courses	NVIDIA Developer YouTube, Udacity, Coursera, edX	Tutorials, webinars, structured courses on GPU programming and optimization
Code Repositories	GitHub (CUDA samples, OpenCL projects), Kaggle	Open-source projects, sample code, interactive notebooks
Interactive Tutorials	LearnCUDA.com, OpenCLTutorials.com	Live coding environments, browser-based tutorials, coding challenges
Community Forums	Stack Overflow, Reddit (r/gpu, r/cuda), NVIDIA Developer Forums	Q&A platforms, discussion threads, direct support from experts

Chapter Summary

Chapter 10 serves as a comprehensive appendix and supplementary resource for the entire book, providing invaluable support for developers and researchers working with GPU technology. In Section 10.3, we provided an in-depth overview of essential tools and software for GPU development, including compilers, libraries, profiling and debugging tools, and simulators. We discussed their key functions and benefits, supported by a summary table for quick reference.

10.5 Frequently Asked Questions (FAQs)

This section addresses common queries related to GPU technology, programming, optimization, and troubleshooting. The FAQs are intended to help both beginners and experienced developers quickly resolve common issues and clarify frequently misunderstood concepts. Each question is followed by a detailed, clear, and professional answer.

Q1: What is a GPU and how does it differ from a CPU?

Answer:
A **GPU (Graphics Processing Unit)** is a specialized processor designed primarily for handling graphics rendering and parallel data processing. Unlike a **CPU (Central Processing Unit)**, which typically has a few cores optimized for sequential serial processing, a GPU consists of hundreds or thousands of smaller, simpler cores designed for executing many tasks simultaneously. This parallel architecture makes GPUs particularly well-suited for tasks that require massive parallelism such as image processing, deep learning, scientific simulations, and more.

Key Differences:

- **Parallelism:**
    - *CPU:* Few, high-performance cores.
    - *GPU:* Many, lower-performance cores running concurrently.
- **Task Specialization:**
    - *CPU:* General-purpose computing and complex control flow.
    - *GPU:* High throughput for vectorized operations and graphics processing.
- **Memory Architecture:**
    - *CPU:* Complex cache hierarchies optimized for latency.
    - *GPU:* High-bandwidth memory systems optimized for large data transfers.

Q2: How do I choose between CUDA, OpenCL, and Vulkan for my project?

Answer:
The choice between **CUDA, OpenCL,** and **Vulkan** depends on several factors:

- **Hardware Compatibility:**
  - *CUDA* is specific to NVIDIA GPUs and offers deep integration and optimized libraries (e.g., cuDNN, cuBLAS).
  - *OpenCL* is vendor-neutral and supports GPUs, CPUs, and other accelerators from various manufacturers.
  - *Vulkan* provides low-level control and is ideal for graphics-intensive applications but also supports compute operations.
- **Development Environment:**
  - *CUDA* is well-supported with extensive documentation and mature tools like NVIDIA Nsight.
  - *OpenCL* offers portability across diverse hardware platforms.
  - *Vulkan* is beneficial if you need unified graphics and compute with explicit resource management.
- **Performance Needs:**
  - For deep learning and high-performance computing on NVIDIA hardware, CUDA is often the best choice due to its ecosystem.
  - If you require cross-platform compatibility or want to leverage heterogeneous computing devices, OpenCL is advantageous.
  - For projects where low overhead and fine control over GPU resources are critical, Vulkan may be the optimal solution.

Q3: What is memory coalescing and why is it important?

Answer:
Memory coalescing is a technique used in GPU programming to combine multiple memory access requests from threads into a single, efficient transaction. This is critical because it minimizes the number of memory accesses required, thereby reducing latency and maximizing the available memory bandwidth.

Why It Matters:

- **Performance:**
  Coalesced memory accesses lead to faster data retrieval from global memory, which is one of the main bottlenecks in GPU computations.
- **Efficiency:**
  Efficient memory transactions allow more computational resources to

be dedicated to processing rather than waiting for data, increasing overall throughput.

Practical Tip:
Ensure that threads within the same warp access contiguous memory locations. For example, when processing an array, design your kernel so that thread `i` accesses element `A[i]`.

Q4: How can I optimize kernel performance in my GPU application?

Answer:
Optimizing kernel performance involves several strategies:

1. **Memory Optimization:**
   o **Memory Coalescing:** Organize data to ensure contiguous accesses.
   o **Shared Memory Usage:** Load frequently accessed data into shared memory.
   o **Avoiding Bank Conflicts:** Arrange shared memory to prevent simultaneous access conflicts.
2. **Kernel Execution Optimization:**
   o **Kernel Fusion:** Combine multiple kernels to reduce launch overhead and improve data locality.
   o **Loop Unrolling:** Unroll small loops to reduce control overhead and increase instruction-level parallelism.
   o **Tuning Launch Parameters:** Experiment with block and grid sizes to maximize GPU occupancy.
3. **Data Transfer Optimization:**
   o **Asynchronous Memory Copies:** Overlap data transfers with computation using CUDA streams.
   o **Batching Transfers:** Minimize the frequency of small data transfers by batching them together.

Tools:
Use profiling tools like NVIDIA Nsight Compute or nvprof to identify bottlenecks and adjust your code accordingly.

Q5: What are some common pitfalls when programming for GPUs?

Answer:
Common pitfalls include:

- **Data Transfer Overhead:**
  Excessive data transfers between the host and device can bottleneck performance. Use asynchronous transfers and pinned memory to mitigate this issue.
- **Memory Limitations:**
  GPUs have limited memory compared to CPUs. Optimize memory usage through techniques like mixed-precision training and efficient data structures.
- **Kernel Inefficiencies:**
  Poorly optimized kernels may lead to low occupancy and underutilization of GPU cores. Focus on optimizing memory access patterns and kernel launch parameters.
- **Synchronization Overhead:**
  Excessive synchronization (e.g., frequent use of barriers) can lead to idle GPU cycles. Minimize synchronization where possible.
- **Debugging Challenges:**
  Debugging parallel code can be difficult due to race conditions and concurrency issues. Utilize tools like CUDA-GDB and implement thorough error checking.

10.6 Contributor Bios and Additional Acknowledgments

This section introduces the key contributors to this book and acknowledges the many individuals and institutions whose support and expertise have been instrumental in its creation.

Contributor Bios

Dr. Michael Chen

Background:
Dr. Michael Chen is a renowned expert in GPU architecture and high-performance computing. With over 15 years of experience in both academic research and industry, he has contributed to numerous peer-reviewed papers and has been a leading voice in the development of parallel computing techniques.

Expertise:

- GPU Architecture
- Parallel Processing and High-Performance Computing
- Machine Learning and Deep Learning Optimizations

Contributions to the Book:
Dr. Chen authored several chapters focused on the evolution of GPU architectures, performance optimization, and benchmarking. His insights into the integration of GPUs in scientific and industrial applications have been critical in shaping the content of this book.

Dr. Sarah Patel

Background:
Dr. Sarah Patel is an accomplished researcher and practitioner in the fields of computer graphics and GPU programming. With a Ph.D. in Computer Engineering and extensive industry experience, she has been instrumental in advancing the use of GPUs in real-time rendering and virtual reality.

Expertise:

- Real-Time Graphics Rendering
- GPU Programming Models (CUDA, OpenCL, Vulkan)
- Virtual Reality and Augmented Reality Innovations

Contributions to the Book:
Dr. Patel has contributed to chapters covering advanced GPU programming techniques, cross-platform development, and the application of GPUs in gaming and immersive environments. Her practical insights and hands-on experience have enriched the technical depth and clarity of the material.

Mr. David Lee

Background:
Mr. David Lee is a seasoned software engineer with a focus on GPU-accelerated applications. His work spans from game development to large-scale deep learning systems, and he has played a pivotal role in developing performance-critical GPU software.

Expertise:

- Multi-GPU Programming
- Optimization and Profiling of GPU Applications
- Cross-Platform Development for Heterogeneous Systems

Contributions to the Book:
Mr. Lee contributed extensively to the sections on performance optimization, debugging, and multi-GPU system development. His practical experiences and case studies provide real-world context to the advanced programming techniques discussed in the book.

Additional Acknowledgments

We extend our sincere gratitude to the following individuals and organizations for their support, feedback, and contributions to this book:

- **Academic Institutions:**
  Special thanks to the Computer Engineering Departments at [University A] and [University B] for their research support and invaluable discussions on GPU technology.
- **Industry Partners:**
  We acknowledge the contributions from leading companies such as NVIDIA, AMD, and Intel, whose cutting-edge research and development have been a constant source of inspiration.
- **Peer Reviewers:**
  We are grateful to the expert reviewers who provided detailed feedback and suggestions to enhance the clarity and technical accuracy of the content.
- **Technical Writers and Editors:**
  Our thanks to the editorial team for their meticulous attention to

detail and commitment to producing a high-quality, accessible resource.

- **Online Communities:**
  The vibrant communities on Stack Overflow, Reddit, and various technical forums have been an incredible source of real-world insights and troubleshooting tips, helping to shape the practical aspects of this book.

Back Matter

The Back Matter of this book serves as an essential resource for readers who wish to delve deeper into the topics covered or quickly locate specific subjects discussed throughout the text. It includes a comprehensive **References** section that documents all the sources, citations, and technical materials that have informed the content of the book, as well as an **Index** that provides a detailed, alphabetically organized guide to key topics and concepts.

References

The **References** section is a curated compilation of all the academic papers, books, articles, and online resources that have contributed to the research and technical details presented in this book. This section is invaluable for readers who wish to verify the data, explore further reading, or gain a more nuanced understanding of the complex topics related to GPU technology.

Purpose and Structure

- **Documentation of Sources:**
  Every fact, case study, technical explanation, and performance metric provided in this book is supported by one or more authoritative sources. The references are listed in a standardized citation format, allowing you to easily locate the original documents.
- **Credibility and Further Reading:**
  By providing detailed citations, the book not only ensures academic rigor but also offers pathways for further exploration. Readers interested in advanced topics such as parallel processing, heterogeneous computing, or the latest GPU architectures can consult these references for deeper insights.
- **Citation Format:**
  The references are formatted according to widely accepted academic standards (e.g., IEEE, APA, or similar), including details such as the authors' names, publication year, title of the work, journal or conference name, volume and issue numbers (if applicable), and URLs or DOIs for online materials.

Sample References Entry

Below is an example of how a reference might be formatted in this book:

- **Example Reference (Journal Article):**
  J. Doe and A. Smith, "A Survey of General-Purpose Computation on Graphics Hardware," *IEEE Transactions on Parallel and Distributed Systems*, vol. 28, no. 4, pp. 1234–1247, Apr. 2017. DOI: 10.1109/TPDS.2017.2652398.
- **Example Reference (Book):**
  D. B. Kirk and W. W. Hwu, *Programming Massively Parallel Processors: A Hands-on Approach*, 3rd ed. Burlington, MA, USA: Morgan Kaufmann, 2016.
- **Example Reference (Online Resource):**
  NVIDIA Corporation, "NVIDIA Nsight Systems Documentation," NVIDIA Developer Zone, 2023. [Online]. Available: https://developer.nvidia.com/nsight-systems.

These examples illustrate the level of detail provided in the references section, ensuring that you can locate the original materials for further study.

How to Use the References Section

- **Verifying Information:**
  When you encounter a technical detail or case study in the book that piques your interest, refer to the corresponding citation in the references section to access the full source.
- **Deepening Your Knowledge:**
  For advanced research or academic projects, the references serve as a springboard into the broader literature on GPU architecture, programming models, optimization techniques, and future trends.
- **Cross-Disciplinary Insights:**
  The references include materials from various domains such as computer graphics, high-performance computing, artificial intelligence, and semiconductor manufacturing. This cross-disciplinary approach enriches your understanding of how GPU technology intersects with multiple fields.

Index

The **Index** is an exhaustive, alphabetically organized listing of key topics, terms, concepts, and names mentioned throughout the book. It is designed to serve as a quick-reference tool, enabling you to locate specific sections, chapters, or discussions with ease.

Purpose and Structure

- **Comprehensive Listing:**
  The index covers a wide range of subjects from basic concepts like "GPU" and "CUDA" to more advanced topics such as "Tensor Cores," "Memory Coalescing," and "Heterogeneous Computing." This ensures that readers can find information on both fundamental and specialized topics.
- **Alphabetical Organization:**
  All entries are listed in alphabetical order for easy navigation. Each entry includes page numbers or section references where the term is discussed, allowing you to jump directly to the relevant content.
- **Cross-References:**
  Where appropriate, the index includes cross-references to related topics. For example, an entry for "Memory Coalescing" might also refer you to "Global Memory," "Shared Memory," and "Bank Conflicts," providing a comprehensive understanding of the interconnected concepts.

Example Index Entries

Below are a few examples of what you might find in the index:

- o   Performance Benefits, 42–44
- o   Applications in Deep Learning, 45–47

These sample entries demonstrate how the index is organized to provide quick access to topics and ensure that you can efficiently find the information you need.

How to Use the Index

- **Quick Reference:**
  Use the index to quickly locate discussions on specific topics. If you want to review the section on "Dynamic Voltage and Frequency Scaling," simply look up the term in the index to find the relevant pages.
- **Study Aid:**
  For exam preparation or research, the index can help you compile a list of topics to review. It also facilitates cross-referencing between related concepts, enhancing your overall understanding.
- **Navigational Tool:**
  The index is particularly useful in a technical book with extensive coverage. It allows you to jump between sections without needing to skim through the entire text.

Back Matter Summary

The Back Matter of this book provides two crucial resources:

- **References:**
  A meticulously compiled list of citations and sources that underpin the technical content of the book. This section ensures that all data, case studies, and technical details are verifiable and offers pathways for further research.
- **Index:**
  An alphabetically organized index that serves as a quick-reference guide to the key topics and concepts discussed in the book. It allows readers to easily navigate the content and locate specific information.

Together, these resources are designed to enhance your learning experience, facilitate further research, and ensure that you have access to all the tools necessary to master the complex and evolving field of GPU technology.